D0732637

Spiritual Dimensions
of
the Martial Arts

Spiritual Dimensions
of
the Martial Arts

Michael Maliszewski, Ph.D.

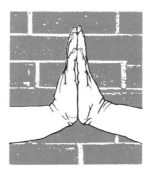

Charles E. Tuttle Company
Rutland, Vermont & Tokyo, Japan

(Frontispiece). *Guro* Dan Inosanto performs the introductory salutation and prayer from the Lacosta Kali system.

DISCLAIMER

Please note that the author and publisher of this book are NOT RESPONSIBLE in any manner whatsoever for any injury that may result from practicing the techniques and/or following the instructions given within. Since the physical activities described herein may be too strenuous in nature for some readers to engage in safely, *it is essential that a physician be consulted prior to training.*

Published by the Charles E. Tuttle Company, Inc.
of Rutland, Vermont & Tokyo, Japan
with editorial offices at
2-6 Suido 1-chome, Bunkyo-ku, Tokyo 112

LCC Card No. 96-60594
ISBN 0-8048-2048-1

First edition, 1996

Printed in Singapore

THIS TEXT is dedicated to the memory of Mircea Eliade. As a scholar of international renown, his friendship, breadth of knowledge, humility, and support over the years served as an ongoing source of encouragement. His comments on an earlier draft of this work were most helpful to completing this research. His death in 1986 was a great personal loss.

❖ Table of Contents ❖

❖ Acknowledgments ❖

THE FORMAL research associated with this book covers a period of ten years, preceded by over a decade of advanced practice and experience in various classical meditative systems and, independently, involvement in a variety of martial arts. Through practice, academic investigations, and personal relationships, I have benefited from interactions with a wide array of practitioners from various martial arts, meditation teachers, academicians, language specialists, and other individuals from divergent backgrounds. Without the cooperation of these people, this work would not have reached its present form. To all of them, I am most grateful for their assistance. Final evaluations of information included in this work as well as positions taken to the subject matter, however, remain my own, and hence, I bear the responsibility for any inaccuracies contained within.

To begin, no writing would have been possible without the practitioners and teachers of various martial arts and the written sources and oral traditions associated with their practices. For their respective contributions, I am especially indebted to the following people: Lokendra Arambam, Dionisio Cañete, William Cheung, Wai Lun Choi, Ken Cohen, Fred Degerberg, John DeJong, James W. DeMile, Gladson de Oliveira Silva, Paul de Thouars, Steven K. Dowd, Bob Duggan, Leo Fong, Michael Fox, Kahn Foxx, Robert Frazer, Leo T. Gaje, Jr., Jesse Glover, Jane Hallander, Paul Harper, Ed Hart, Stephen K. Hayes, Adam Hsu, Joe Hyams, Shishir Inocalla, Dan Inosanto, Suryadi (Eddy) Jafri, Halford E. Jones, Thomas Kelham, Nongmaithem Khilton, Chang Sik Kim, Maria Rowe Kim, Taky Kimura, Ben Largusa, Joo Bang Lee, Benjamin Pang Jeng Lo, Al McLuckie, Peter Moy, John P. Painter, Marcello Pereira, Jhoon Rhee, R. K. Priya Gopal Sana, Guido Schauer, C. Mohammed Sherif, Sang Kyu Shim, Surachai Sirisute, John Stewart, and In Hyuk Suh. To this list of practitioners, I add my gratitude to my first instructors in the martial arts: Jeffrey Baker, Dale Pfeiffer, and Clayton Cortes.

A number of scholars from a variety of divergent disciplines have assisted in tracking down elusive writings, clarifying ambiguous issues, or generally outlining position statements within their respective area of study. For their assistance, I wish to thank the following individuals: Ben Anderson, Olfar Bragason, Don Calhoun, Larry Chalip, Nancy Cirillo, Jonathan Cohen, Jean Comaroff, Richard T. Curley, Edward Dimock, Jr., Clifford Geertz, Paul Griffiths, Herbert Guenther, H. Isler, Rev. Jikai (Choffy), Chong Sun Kim, Winston L. King, Kinoshita Hideaki, Joseph Kitagawa, T. C. Koh, Stanley Krippner, Ya-Guang Liu, Michael J. Mahoney, Niels Mulder, Lati Rinbochay, Arion Rosu, Brent S. Rushall, John M. Silva III, Michael Smith, Frits Staal, Paul Stange, Brendall Suyenobu, Uzawa Yoshiyuki, Robert Weinberg, Rhea White, and L. R. T. Williams.

Additional thanks and attention are due those individuals who have combined practice with academic and research investigations: Daniel Amos, Hunter (Chip) Armstrong, Jerry Beasley, Hiltrud Cordes, Catherine Evleshin, Bernard Faure, Arnold M. Golub, David A. Hall, Lester Ingber, Alan James, He-Young Kimm, Ken Kushner, Donald Levine, J. Lowell Lewis, Patrick Lineberger, Dave Lowry, Dirk Mosig, Thomas Nardi, V. Pandian, Howard Pashenz, Mike Sayama, Robert W. Smith, Hardy Stockmann, Shizuo Tanaka, Eugene Taylor, Dwight Tkatschow, Michael Trulson, David B. Waterhouse, Douglas Wile, Mark V. Wiley, and Phillip Zarrilli.

I am indebted to those individuals with a background or specialization in many of the foreign languages included in this text who often gave generously of their time, assisting me in translating and verifying esoteric and highly specialized terms, and further adapting their written form to acceptable standards of romanization: William J. Alspaugh, Idelma Baro, Olfar Bragason, Suk-In Chang, John Chathanatt, Gay Young Cho, Kong Kyu Choo, Bruce Craig, Inge de la Camp, Lollie Delrosario, Michael A. DeMarco, June Farris, Cai Fung-Pei, Vijayarani Fedson, Linda Fernandez, Jeanne Harbour, Scott Edward Harrison, Mulyadi Kartanegara, Sri Sadeli Kuhns, Tai-Loi Ma, Juni Manow, Steven Michaud, Christa Modschiedler, Linda Moore, Eizaburo Okuizumi, Halyna Pankiw, Maureen Patterson, Robert A. Petersen, Lili Rabel-Heymann, Clarita Raghunanan, A. K. Ramanujan, Frank Reynolds, Mani Reynolds, Rod Rojas, Somi Roy, Martha Selby, Paul Sprachman, Jaroslav Stetkevych, Parichart Suwanbubbha, Beth Vinkler, Doug Wile, Young-Jin Yang, and Tim Wong.

Additional assistance was also provided by Norman Borine, Steve Diamond, Steve Donovan, Marshall Frankel, Lilia Howe, Jason Kaplan, Linda Lee, James Nail, Iris P. Sachs, Sandra Segal, and Geri Simon.

Special thanks also go to Barbara Vaughan who initially urged me, with some prodding at the early stages of speculation, to commit my findings, observations, and experiential insights to print. Finally, I am indebted to Michael A. DeMarco for publishing an earlier academic version of this work and Mark V. Wiley who assisted in the final preparation of this text.

❖ Introduction ❖

Romanization Systems, Spelling Styles, and Name Designations

For each of the non-Western languages in the text, a specific system of romanization was initially used for the academic version. For Chinese, the Pinyin system has been employed for Mandarin words, while Sidney Lau's system of romanization has been used for Cantonese terms. In Japanese, the modified Hepburn style is used, with word division being determined by current Library of Congress practices. For Korean, the McCune-Reischauer system has been followed. Though the systems used for the Sanskrit and Tagalog languages lack specific names, the most contemporary and standard systems of romanization have been followed. Indonesian and Javanese orthography reflect the spelling changes announced by the Indonesian government in 1972. The Thai language follows the style of romanization devised by the Royal Institute of Bangkok in 1954. The remaining languages and dialects follow the most current and generally accepted romanization/spelling styles (where applicable, the Library of Congress form). Minor changes were later made by the publisher to accommodate the format used by this press. However, bibliographic references appear in the form in which they were published, even if this is at variance with the systems of romanization and spelling styles found in the body of the text.

The names of individuals found in the main text and footnotes appear as follows: Individuals of the Western world have their names written in anglicized form with first name followed by last name. For Chinese, Japanese, or Korean names, the general rule has been to follow Oriental usage in name order—surname is first and given name is second. In a case where a person is known by several names (e.g., in China, a courtesy name [zi]), I have used the name by which he or she appears to be most commonly known. Where an individual has become known or published in the English-speaking world under a particular name, that name will be used.

Abbreviations

A number of foreign language entries appear within this text. As a general rule, an entry in a foreign language will be followed by the name of the language in abbreviated form. This entry will often be accompanied by its English translation. The abbreviation is not designated in those sections where it is clear that a single language (already identified) is being used. Those languages and dialects that are seldom referred to within this book have been identified and spelled out in their entirety. Languages for which abbreviations have been used include: Sanskrit (Skt.), Spanish (Span.), Tagalog (Tag.), Visayan (Vis.), Korean (Kor.), Malayalam (Mal.), Manipuri (Manip.), Portuguese (Port.), Mandarin Chinese (Chin. or Chin./M.), Cantonese Chinese (Chin./C.), Indonesian (Ind.), Japanese (Jpn.), and Javanese (Jav.). If the foreign word entry appears in the main text, then the abbreviation will follow immediately. If the word appears within parentheses, then the abbreviation will be listed at the end.

Notes on References

An overwhelming majority of writings dealing strictly with the martial arts are of poor academic quality. Those works concerned with the history of martial arts are generally uncritical in their treatment and poorly referenced. Most books are concerned with techniques and movements that characterize the physical aspects of a particular martial art. Here, too, proponents of a respective style may argue about the accuracy of the information presented in the particular work dealing with their art. Articles appearing in various commercial magazines may contain information of a historical, technique-oriented, or philosophical focus, but are generally even more limited and superficial than material that appears in book format. (See listings in Corcoran and Farkas [1983] and Nelson [1988] for a range of contemporary published works in English.) These articles are in direct contrast to many writings that appear in established academic disciplines such as anthropology, history of religions, or South Asian studies, that are of superior scholarship.

In an attempt to draw together the literature of the seemingly disparate fields of martial arts and meditative-religious traditions, one is faced with the need to select various sources to document information presented, yet simultaneously is limited by the quality of works available. I have attempted to document as carefully as possible and critically assess all information presented herein though the conclusions reached stem from my own speculations and experiences in various martial arts and meditative traditions. To this end, a significant percentage of information presented here will be based on original research derived from extensive studies and interviews I conducted in the United States and abroad. With the exception of the martial arts of China and Japan, most of the discussion of meditation, spiritual practices, and religious goals associated with various martial arts will appear in print for the first time. In a number of cases, it has taken several years to track down teachers and masters of these disciplines and to then gain access to information not available to the general public. Even more time elapsed as I attempted to verify such information. The reader interested in an earlier academic treatment of this subject and commentary with an extensive bibliography is referred to my previous writing (see Maliszewski, 1992c). Additional essays on this subject also appear in subsequent issues of the *Journal of Asian Martial Arts.*

With respect to written sources, those writings that deal with the cultural, psychological, religious, or meditative literature are of high quality (unless identified otherwise). In the case of martial arts literature proper, three types of source material have been used: 1. texts that cover historical and contemporary status of martial traditions and are generally of very high quality; 2. books that outline and illustrate through pictorial-sequential and narrative forms the physical movements and techniques of a particular martial art and that generally range from average to high quality; and 3. magazine articles, ranging from fair to satisfactory quality, that serve to illustrate or document credible information not contained in primary literature sources.

To assist the reader in evaluating the quality of reference sources for contemporary martial arts, the best references have been identified in the reference section of this text. It is hoped that as an increasing number of scholars become involved in this area of research (academically as well as through direct, experiential participation), the quality of martial-based source material will likewise improve, approaching a level of sophistication comparable to that of other academic disciplines.

PART ONE

A Contemporary Assessment
of
Martial Arts

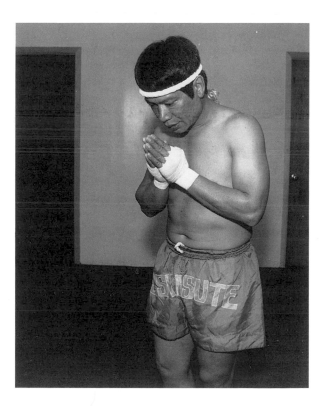

Without the tempering effects of religious values, no system of self-defense can rise above sheer acts of rowdy violence.

—Quintin Chambers and Donn F. Draeger

He who wishes to live in an oriental martial art, rather than to just practice it on a physical level, must so train his consciousness to attain a self-discipline that at last his conscious mind will merge into an identity with the very principle of life itself.

—Maurice Zalle

(Overleaf). *Aa-chan* Surachai Sirisute at the completion of the *ram-muay* prefight ritual dance.

THE HISTORY of combat is as old as man himself, its origins lost in the passage of time. Forms of combat have been extremely varied throughout history, but in Asia reached a level of sophistication, complexity, and effectiveness seldom matched in other parts of the world. Religious beliefs and teachings interpenetrated many of these martial arts—a factor that often distinguished them from their Western counterparts. This association is the subject of this book.

Today and particularly within the last fifteen years, there has been increased public interest in various forms of self-defense. In particular, Asian methods of self-defense imported from such countries as China, Japan, Korea, Okinawa, and the Philippines have, by and large, received the greatest attention in America and Europe. The attraction of people to these martial arts has been based on a number of different factors, among the foremost being: 1. their applicability as a form of self-defense; 2. a means of achieving self-discipline; 3. an outlet for aggression; 4. a method of conquering physical fears and anxieties that emanate from living in a hostile environment; 5. a means of physical exercise and conditioning; 6. a source of social and environmental support; 7. a method of increasing one's level of self-esteem and confidence; and 8. a method of achieving power and mastery by performing seemingly impossible feats of speed, strength, and agility.

The focus of practitioners and writers involved in these Eastern disciplines has been varied and wide in scope. This is best illustrated by writings that have appeared in numerous books and popular (U.S.) magazines such as the *Journal of Asian Martial Arts, Aikido Journal, Furyu, Black Belt, Martial Arts Training, Karate/Kung-Fu Illustrated, Inside Kung-Fu, Inside Karate, Inside Tae Kwon Do, Tae Kwon Do Times, Wushu Kung-Fu, Budo Dojo, Mudo Dojang,* and *Qi.* Among the many topics explored and discussed by serious practitioners have been: 1. the nature and importance of "intrinsic energy" (Chin., *qi;* Jpn., Kor., *ki;* Skt., *prana*) in the martial arts as well as the different ways this "energy" is used by varying styles; 2. the comparative-analytic stance taken toward the evaluation and application of specific offensive or defensive techniques in various martial arts; 3. the use of traditional, regimented, prearranged sets of forms (Chin., *quan;* Jpn., *kata;* Kor., *hyong*) as a preparation for self-defense maneuvers versus those systems that avoid the use of pre-set exercises and response patterns; 4. the use of circular movements in self-defense strategies versus those strategies emphasizing a direct, linear approach; 5. the role of biomechanical principles; 6. the use of traditional techniques of self-defense characterized by a particular style that notably emerged from a particular country and time period versus those of a more transcultural, eclectic form that integrate a number of different yet current styles; 7. the importance of developing speed, timing, and strategy in fighting techniques; 8. the merits of various approaches in regard to learning martial arts techniques; and 9. the relevance of the martial arts to education.[1]

All of the above-mentioned areas have been of great concern to practitioners of martial arts. Seriously missing, however, has been the emphasis placed upon the psychological authentication or transformation associated with these various physical activities through involvement in meditative-religious practices. This omission is surprising in light of the fact that at different historical periods the teachings and principles of many martial arts were influenced by various meditative disciplines and "physicalistic exercise" schools that embraced metaphysical teachings of various religions and placed importance upon psychological changes within the practitioner.[2] Occasionally, the terminology of the Asian philosophies is espoused by practitioners or writers in the field today. However, they are usually used in a superficial or inaccurate fashion (historically, linguistically, psychologically, and philosophically). Essentially, the depth of association that many of these disciplines had with specific religious traditions has gone unrecognized. It is not uncommon to find martial arts teachers focusing on the physical aspects of the art to the detriment or exclusion of the philosophical, religious, or spiritual side. The result is often a vigorous self-defense art that has become alienated from its rich historical background and true origins.

Ironically, this has occurred precisely at a time when interest in consciousness studies has expanded into more traditional disciplines, such as the history of religions, Asian studies, psychology, biology, medicine, and anthropology, and also at a time of increased interest in physical exercise as a means of enhancing physical and mental well-being. It is rather puzzling to note that no one involved in those academic disciplines that are most directly concerned with the topic of human consciousness has seriously explored the meditative dimensions of the martial arts, where the synthesis of an already established philosophical-religious-experiential base has existed concurrent with the emphasis placed upon physical development and health. The lack of serious attention by practitioners of these disciplines to the meditative-religious dimension of their tradition as well as scholars' lack of attention to or participation in the martial arts is a central theme addressed in this book.

There is little doubt that methodological and procedural difficulties abound when attempts are made to relate martial exercises to religious-philosophical underpinnings. On the topic of religion, attempts to define words such as "meditation" or even "religion" itself are invariably inadequate. Some writers have argued that such terms cannot be defined,[3] whereas most writings will generally concede that no single definition, approach, or set of criteria can incorporate all of the varied forms in which meditation or religion appear.[4] For purposes of this writing, the descriptive words "meditative," "religious," "spiritual," and related terminology, are used in a psychological and phenomenological fashion to refer to those experiences that alter the individual's customary experience and awareness of himself in the world. Varying among the major religious traditions (which often serve as referents for their descriptive characteristics), such experiences can be theistic or non-theistic, individual or group, passive or active, transitory or enduring, intense or mild, expected or spontaneous, novel or recurring, and tradition-centered or not. They may also be viewed as revelational, insightful, confirming, responsive, mystical, ecstatic, and transformative, though other descriptors also exist.[5] Reference to religions and religious traditions have been applied to those systems of belief or worship that incorporate such phenomena, historically or in a more contemporary fashion, within their teachings or philosophical premises. "Meditation" has generally referred to those practices that involve the focusing of attention non-analytically in either a concentrated or expansive fashion, the outcome of which can lead to an alteration in consciousness, an increase in awareness and insight, or a combination of such psychological factors. Many classical meditative systems have an experiential goal associated with the completion of the spiritual path, commonly described as "enlightenment." In contrast to the above-mentioned psychological factors, which can relatively easily emerge from the practice of meditation, the experiential facets of enlightenment are viewed as effecting a radical, oftentimes enduring, psychological authentication (i.e., realizing that which one really is, completely, at all times)[6] or transformation (developing latent capabilities), dramatically affecting the nature of consciousness and changing an individual's behavior in the world as well. The term "enlightenment" generally refers to the complete realization of the true nature of reality, freed from ignorance, illusion, misinformation, cultural biases, and conditioned beliefs. The use of the term "spiritual" has been used to connote the nature of spirit, the sacred, or supernatural. The goals associated with the practice of classical meditative systems, however, may or may not be described as "religious," "spiritual," or "meditative" in nature and must be assessed individually within a respective school, tradition, or religion.

Aside from semantic considerations posed by religious and meditative terms, criteria for what constitutes authentic martial traditions must also be addressed. While the designation of "martial art" is widely used today to refer to a variety of South Asian, Southeast Asian, and Far Eastern combat systems, many of these disciplines would not, by strict definition, be considered genuine martial arts. Researchers seriously involved in the study of man's combative culture define martial arts as systems of combat that primarily involve the use of specialized weapons and protective equipment and facilities for battlefield use developed by and for a professional group of warriors for the ultimate purpose of group solidarity and survival adaptation. In many cases, the professional warrior belonged to a privileged aristocratic and hereditary social class that engaged in a life of discipline and activities connected with all aspects of the combative realm. Contrasting these martial arts is the collection of fighting systems known as civilian arts. Civilian arts are devised by heterogeneous social units in the plebeian segments of society. They are primarily used as methods of self-defense, not related to battlefield conditions, and may or may not make use of weapons or protective equipment and facilities. Further categorizations may be made with respect to sport-oriented or spiritualistic systems, which would not be classified as authentically "martial" in nature.[7] As is generally the case today, more common non-academic writings that review Asian combat systems subsume such disciplines within the designation of martial art, referring to them as simply styles of combat originating in the Orient that offer a way of life based on Eastern philosophy.[8] In still other reviews, however, no such classification or definition even appears in print.[9] No definitions of martial art or martial discipline *per se* appear in general English dictionaries. However, related terms can be found: "Martial" (derived from the Latin word, *martialis,* dedicated to Mars, god of war) means "inclined to the circumstances of war or battle or serving as training for warfare." "Military" (as opposed to civil; adapted from the Latin word, *militaris,* formed on *milit-,* miles, soldier) suggests whatever pertains to a soldier. A "fight" (from Old English, *fechte, foeht;* Old Saxon, Old High German, *fehta;* Middle High German, *vehte*) refers to a hostile encounter, engagement, or combat between two or more people. "Combat" (adapted from the Old French verb, *combatre,* to fight with) constitutes an encounter or fight between two armed persons. "War" (from Old English, *wyrre, werre;* Old High German, *werra,* Middle High German, *werre;* Old Saxon, *werran,* confusion, discord) is a hostile contention by means of armed forces, carried on between nations, states, or rulers or between parties in the same nation or state.[10]

Precise terminology proposed by serious researchers should be considered in any investigation of classical or contemporary martial traditions. However, close inspection of teachings, practices, and/or philosophical premises adhered to by systems falling within the above designations indicate divergent meanings of important terms. As a result, distinct classifications and boundaries will not necessarily hold true or remain internally consistent in all cases. To this end, the simplistic designations found in popular writings may, surprisingly, be viewed as somewhat less superfluous than what was initially suspected. The complexity of this state of affairs becomes more obvious when martial-based systems are explored cross-culturally and historically. The classification proposed earlier will also vary with respect to the designation a specific culture, country, or tradition applies to a particular martial system.

For purposes of this present work, the designation of martial art will be applied to those comprehensive systems of combat or self-defense that may involve unarmed tactics as well as the use of weapons and, either historically or on the contemporary scene, derive their roots or teachings from combat systems designated as such within their respective cultural or geographical settings. Some of these systems will be found to have a more limited association with the combative sphere, as the primary goal involves a radical psychological authentication or transformation of the individual. However, one assumption is that all systems discussed herein have some form of physical training that hypothetically could be used in a combative context. In contrast, formal meditative systems (which they may resemble) generally do not have this combative aspect within their realm of practice.

In addition to issues of terminology, additional methodological and procedural concerns emerge when meditative practices are discussed with respect to martial arts. For certain countries, such as Japan and China, an analysis of classical religious texts, historical writings, or *densho* (Jpn., transmission scroll) with underlying martial ideologies or philosophies is a task of many years' work even if confined to specific cultures and time periods. In some traditions (e.g., certain Japanese systems), resorting to texts for either analysis of meditative-religious experience, enlightenment or related phenomena, and the nature of the martial way, written expression is generally viewed as inadequate in conveying the essence of either realm of activity. In other cases, some of the martial arts have changed over the years so that metaphysical principles underlying performance of movements (in conjunction with specific mental or meditative exercises) would bear no direct relation to current practices. Further, a number of martial arts are of relatively recent development (e.g., Aikido, Jeet Kune Do) and, though based in part upon classical concepts, offer new insights into the use of psychophysical principles not outlined in the available classical literature. In still other situations, much information concerning the principles and practice of various martial arts was veiled in secrecy (e.g., Capoeira, Kali, Kuntao) and often passed along lines of oral tradition or through seemingly innocuous dance movements. In many cases, the information was exclusive to certain lineages (e.g., select systems of Chinese *gong-fu* and Japanese *ryu*) and only recently has been open to people of Caucasian descent. Finally, in some traditions, the physical aspects of the system may be documented in the classical literature while the experiential-religious dimensions are preserved in oral tradition (e.g., [Togakure-ryu] Ninjutsu). Still other arts have traditionally had no textual basis for their discipline whatsoever (e.g., the Hawaiian martial art of Lua). With respect to actual practice and the experiential facets of the discipline, many teachers will only reveal practical and spiritual dimensions of their tradition to individuals who seriously commit to study for many years, arguing (justifiably) that such teachings can only be understood by direct participation and dedicated practice in the martial system itself.

The purpose of this book is to explore the relationship of martial arts to meditative-religious and spiritual traditions. Particular emphasis is given to the nature of radical psychological authentication or transformation in those martial arts having associations with meditative-religious practices and spiritual traditions. Spiritual tenets and goals held by a number of the classical and contemporary martial arts are reviewed, tracing the development of these disciplines historically. An analysis of the current relationship between the martial arts and meditative-religious traditions is also examined. Finally, directives are offered to integrate these two fields of study drawing upon past historical associations and emergent possibilities reflective of sociocultural and psychological trends existing today.

Note: Complete information regarding each of the following sources can be found in the Bibliography, which begins on p. 143.

[1] see Maliszewski, 1992c
[2] see Huard and Wong, 1997
[3] Webb, 1916
[4] see Crim, Bullard, and Shinn, 1981; Maliszewski, Twemlow, Brown and Engler, 1981
[5] Crim, Bullard, and Shinn, 1981
[6] see Cook, 1983
[7] see Draeger, 1980b, 1981b; "The Martial Concept," 1980; Lineberger, 1988; and Paul, 1979/1980
[8] Corcoran and Farkas, 1983
[9] Quick, 1973
[10] *The Oxford English Dictionary*, 1933

Martial Arts
A Descriptive and Visual Survey

Even if one has learned all the sayings of the sages and saints, he should not insist on them obstinately.

—Toshikaga Asakura

Whenever the doctrine of bujutsu attempts to claim the lofty beliefs of the Oriental doctrines of enlightenment as the inspirational motivations underlying the practice of the martial arts, it must be observed that to proclaim one's adherence to these values in theory and to live up to them in practice . . . are two entirely different things.

—Oscar Ratti and Adele Westbrook

(Overleaf). Sifu Yang Qingyu demonstrating the two-hand push technique from a traditional Yang Taijiquan form.

IT HAS BEEN suggested that hunting skills constituted the preliminary forms of combat for primitive man. When such techniques were pitted against members of his own species, their degree of sophistication likewise increased.[1] However, the origins of the martial arts remain speculative, nebulous, and open to controversy among writers and historians.[2] While no definitive answers will probably be forthcoming, respected scholars generally concede that some of the earliest traceable roots of meditative-religious teachings interpenetrating martial practices and ideologies lead either to India or China. It is beyond the scope of this work to explore the issue further; suffice to say that any legitimate scholarship exploring this topic would take many years' work to sufficiently address our knowledge of this matter.

---

[1] Draeger and Smith, 1969   [2] see Maliszewski, 1992c

MANY CONTEMPORARY surveys of the Asian martial arts fail to provide any detailed information concerning martial practices of India. This is not surprising as many specialists will concede that Indian martial traditions are difficult to locate and verify. While they continue to develop, they have become increasingly rare.[1] Historically, fighting sequences are described in such classic epics as the *Mahabharata, Ramayana,* and the *Rigveda* as well as other religious texts such as the *Buddhacarita Sutra, Jaiminiya Brahmana,* and *Saddharmapundarika Sutra.* Very little is known about these early practices, which preceded the beginnings of Buddhism (500 B.C.).[2] Later written records or texts specific to select martial arts do exist.[3] However, most modern, readily available texts describe the wrestling forms (Binot, Kusthi, Masti, Vajra-musti, Skt.)[4] and weaponry (e.g., *cilampam,* Tamil; *bana, lathi, pata, phari-gatka,* Skt.).[5] Given the limited material available concerning these martial arts, one must look to Indian ideas of the body to uncover information concerning martial traditions,[6] particularly in relation to meditative-religious practices.[7] The most notable sources include Ayurvedic medicine and Yoga (especially Hatha Yoga), which stress the importance of physical well-being as well as the goal of liberation *(moksa).* In the above mentioned yogic tradition, one finds reference to *pratyahara, cakra,* and the raising of the *kundalini* as a means to effecting liberation (see Glossary); the Ayurvedic literature makes mention of *marman,* vulnerable points of the human body.[8] Knowledge of the "vulnerable points" found an application in the practice of wrestling—both martial and therapeutic—as well as in organized systems of armed and unarmed combat existing today in Kerala (southwest India) and Tamilnadu (south and southeast India).[9]

One fighting art that has been studied to some degree, also found in Kerala, is the discipline known as Kalarippayattu (Mal., *kalari,* [idiomatic] fencing school; *payattu,* fencing exercise; *kalarippayattu,* place where martial exercises are performed). Dating back to the twelfth century A.D., many current techniques in the art remain similar to those

1

found in earlier times. In its heyday between the fifteenth and seventeenth centuries, Kalarippayattu constituted a regular component of education for Kerala's martial caste (Nairs). Later, its practice crossed both caste and religious affiliation to include higher caste Yatra Brahmans and lower caste Tiyyas as well as many Muslims and Christians.[10] Depending on the practitioner's religious orientation, specific prayers are performed prior to the commencement of formal Kalarippayattu training. In the Muslim Kalarippayattu tradition, for example, prayers are offered to Allah and past masters of the art involving prayers known as *aya* (Arabic) and *fatiha* (Fig. 1). Such prayers constitute a meditation which calms the mind and warms up the entire body before vigorous training begins. The practice ends in the same manner by performing *salat,* a prayer used to cool down the body and mind. Another method of warming up the body for training is the annual full body massage known as *uliccal* (Mal.), which is administered to practitioners during the cyclical monsoon season.

During one's preliminary training, foundations of this physical culture system consist of individual body exercising sequences known collectively as *meyppayattu.* For example, the *puttara tolil* is a body exercise in which the guardian deity of the *kalari* is worshipped. It is ritually performed at the onset of training. The practitioner performs the exercise by touching the base of the *puttara*, his forehead, and chest (Figs. 2–3), while assuming various body postures. From a martial arts point of view, the physical aspects of the system consist of body poses, steps

2

3

characterized by low stances and long strides, high kicks and jumps, and extended arm and hand movements. The later introduction of weapons such as the *kettukari* (twelve-span staff) (Fig. 4), *ceruvati* (three-span short stick), *otta* (a curved tusk-shaped weapon), *parica* (shield), and *val* (cane staff) adds the use of thrusts, cuts, and evasive moves to the complex repertoire of bodily movements that characterize the art.[11]

Training in Kalarippayattu also has an internal *(antaram)* component. In-depth knowledge of the *marman* (Skt.; *marmmam*, Mal.) is required for purposes of knowing vulnerable points of attack on the opponent (in either empty hand or armed combat), protection of one's own body, and treatment of injuries to the vital spots in training or battle. The emphasis placed upon visual concentration, use of breathing exercises (*pranayama*, Skt., or *swasam*, Mal.), accompanied by special hand-body configurations (*mudra*, Skt.), repetition of *mantra*, economy of movement and energy, and performance of special rituals (paying respects to teachers, deities, and even one's opponent) all aid in achieving proper mind-body coordination.[12] Depicted here is Vasu *Gurukkal* demonstrating special breathing practices that are accompanied by a series of gestural manipulations of the hands (Fig. 5).

Regular pursuit of these practices may lead to the development of power *(sakti)* and a state of "accomplishment" *(siddhi)* in which the doer and done are one.[13] The flow of *prana-vayu* (vital energy: *prana*, breath of life; *vayu*, vital wind) and the initiation of movement from the

4

5

lower abdominal region known as the *nabhi* or *nabhi mula,* correspond-ing to the second yogic *cakra, svadhisthana,* play a significant role in this process.[14]

A number of similarities emerge when some of the techniques and practices employed in various styles *(sampradaya)* of Kalarippayattu arc compared with those found in Yoga. Traditionally in India, how-ever, there is little conscious attention on the part of the practitioner directed to personal changes that may occur as the practice unfolds. To this end, the process of spiritual emancipation *(moksa)* has historically been reserved for the discipline of Yoga. Although there is often an overlap in actual practice among individuals, an intellectual demarcation sepa-rating the two disciplines is common. Therefore, it is not surprising to find some teachers of Kalarippayattu stating there are few, if any, spir-itual components within the system, whereas others definitely see Kala-rippayattu practice as involving spiritual aspects. Teachers of Kalarippayattu *(gurukkal,* Mal.) adhering to this latter position make clear distinctions between their art and Yoga. Yoga is held to be the supreme *sadhana* (Skt., practice) whose aim is explicitly spiritual. Kala-rippayattu is a very physical and active form in which movements per-formed within the discipline of practice serve to exemplify the dynamic tension between control and release.[15] In contrast, Yoga is viewed as stationary and "inactive." One point of agreement between the two practices that Kalarippayattu masters familiar with Yoga share is that both disciplines develop "single point" concentration (ekagrata). Some masters even view the experience of practice as moving even further inward to more subtle, refined, and stationary levels of meditation, i.e., to dharana and eventually dhyana where the "object" of meditation (e.g., the deity) is transcended and a more complete state of non-duality is experienced.[16] However, both paths are traditionally viewed as having their own defining characteristics and place within the Indian social structure. Nonetheless, exceptions to the usual physical/spiritual delineation do exist within certain schools of Kalarippayattu as demonstrated by the conceptual understanding of the body within the art.

Three operative levels of the body are assumed in the practice of Kalarippayattu. The first level is the body as a "vessel" containing humors and saps that determine health by their fluid process of exchange. The second level is essentially a superstructure that supports the vessel, i.e., the bones, muscles, and junctures (marman) of the body. The third level is the subtle interior body assumed generally to be encased within the gross physical body. It is an ideational construct that identifies and articulates internal experience in the psychophysical practice of various sadhana. The first two concepts of the body can be traced to Ayurveda and are generally viewed as two inextricably interrelated aspects of the gross physical body (sthula sarira). The concept and inner alchemy of the subtle body (suksma sarira) evolved separately from Ayurveda as part of ascetic and Yoga practices and appeared fully developed in the Yoga Upanishads and Tantras (after the eighth century A.D.).[17]

It is within the subtle body that reference to such structural elements as nadi, cakra, prana-vayu, and kundalini appear. While formal distinctions between Yoga and Kalarippayattu do exist as noted earlier, some Kalarippayattu master texts do contain descriptions of the conventional seven cakra, select nadi (e.g., ida, pingala, susumna), prana-vayu, and kundalini. Masters who follow such texts may not explain such elements as cakra or kundalini to the student, but do observe the effect of raising the kundalini that may possibly emerge naturally through correct practice. (It is important to note that the student himself may not be aware of the psychophysical process unfolding.) Other texts and teachers, in contrast, make limited reference to these structural elements and may neither recognize nor use the complete map of the subtle body (for example, limiting discussion to the martial arts practitioner controlling prana-vayu and, in turn, the mind). Of note, a proportionate number of Muslim, Christian, and Hindu teachers assume and articulate the subtle body within their practices. Still other teachers make use of a number of meditative techniques that are not a part of traditional Kalarippayattu to improve the student's power of concentration and the ability to control the mind consciously. These may include sitting meditation *(dhyana)* in which the mind is concentrated on the image of a particular deity *(murti)*.[18]

While these divergent trends illustrate the various degrees to which meditative components of practice are pursued, it should be noted that strong emphasis is placed upon spiritual training and development by Sufi Kalarippayattu practitioners of the Cannanore area of northern Kerala. Once the adept has reached higher levels of practice and has gained absolute mastery of the body, oral lessons are provided, including progression through a series of *dhikr* (Arabic), which are techniques of remembrance or recollection of God performed silently or aloud. To develop spiritual power collectively, a ritual group practice known as *ratib* may be performed in which *dhikr* are repeated in unison by the Sufi martial arts practitioners.

Depicted here is the four stage progression of *ratib*. The first stage shows the *ratib* commencement with master and students sitting in a group (Fig. 6). The second stage involves master and students conducting *dhikr*, a meditation/breathing regimen making use of seven different

6

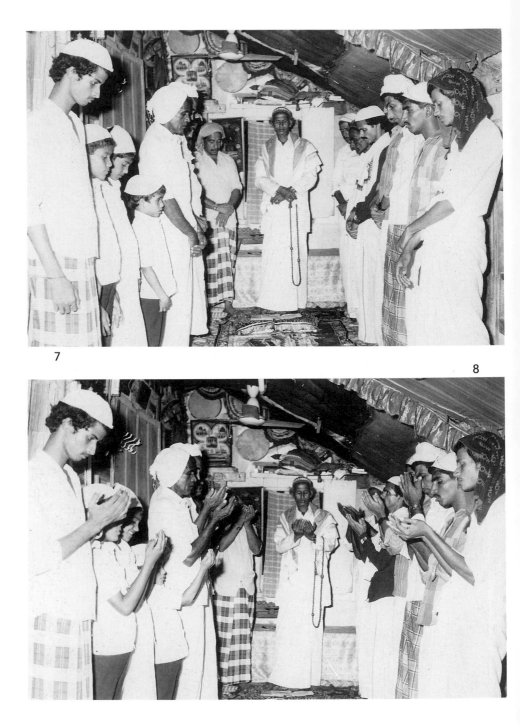

7

8

cakra in the human body (Fig. 7). Prayers are offered in the third stage (Fig. 8). In the final stage, the Sufi master gives *kheerani*, the food of *ratib* (Fig. 9).

Practice of these techniques is understood to have a practical effect on martial arts performance including increased mental and physical strength, concentration, and breath control. Eventually, a state of ecstasy, realization of the internal white light, or union with Allah may be among the types of experiences attained. For such practitioners, the spiritual path constitutes the means by which accomplishment in fighting art practice and union with God are achieved.[19] Nonetheless, this emphasis is a relatively rare exception today.

Another martial art exhibiting similar parallels to Kalarippayattu is Thang-Ta. Thang-Ta (Manip., *thang,* sword; *ta,* spear) is a martial art found in Manipur (northeast India) which consists of animal-like movements and bears some similarities to Kalarippayattu. It involves the practice of forms *(khong'lol-khut'lol)* and use of unarmed techniques (e.g., kicks, punches) as well as weapons such as the dagger *(hak'thang thang)*, spear *(ta)*, broadsword *(thang'jou)*, bow *(ten)*, and dart *(aram-*

9

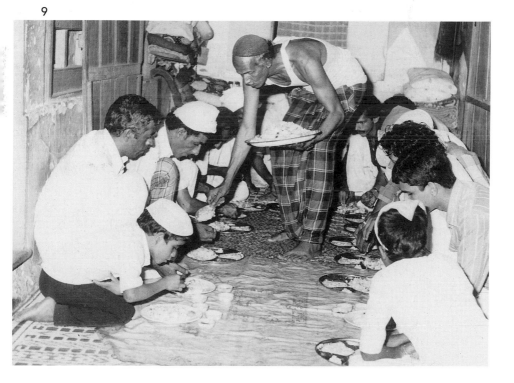

10

bai) (Fig. 10). Saritsarat is a component of Thang-Ta that consists of empty-hand fighting that relies upon footwork and evasion of an opponent's strike by stepping aside in order to add to the momentum of his strike so that he both misses his target and is thrown forward and off-balance.[20] Muk'na is a Manipuri style of wrestling and sub-system of Thang-Ta that involves throwing techniques using hips, shoulders, and legs.

The current forms of martial-meditative and religious practice in Thang-Ta bear many similarities to many schools in the art of Kala-rippayattu. The name of the art itself is closely allied with religious concepts. Thang is represented by Pakhangba, god of the sword; Ta is represented by Ashiba (Sanamahi), the god of the spear. Prior to fighting, rituals involving salutation to one's master *(oja khurumba)* and praying to the deities *(lai khurumba)* are performed. Distinctions are made between physical training *(mapan'gi kang'lol)* and internal training *(nung'gi kang'lol)*. The use of *lairol* (Skt., *mantra*) and *khut'lol* (Skt., *mudra*) can be found. A breathing system *(ningsha-kang'lol)* is practiced in part to cultivate and accumulate internal energy *(ting)* in the lower part of the navel *(channing)*. Reference to mystical physiological concepts may appear that parallel those described earlier such as: *ingla* (Skt., *ida*), *pingla* (Skt., *pingala*), *marong-khong* (Skt., *susumna*), and *pap'hal* (Skt., *kundalini*). However, distinctions between the goals of Yoga and Thang-Ta are clear. Meditative practices are employed by the Thang-Ta practitioner to enter a deep state of concentration *(puk'ning loop'na)* by focusing on the point between the eyebrows so as to effect proper mind-body coordination.

An example of a meditative posture found in Thang-Ta is the *kong'grai achouba* (greater cross-legged stance) (Fig. 11). The practitioner places both hands at the navel, palms up, right hand on top of left hand. As part of internal training *(nung'gi kang'lol)*, meditation is used to extend the internal power and involves one point concentration at a point below the navel *(channing)* while a system of breathing *(ningsha-kang'lol)* is performed.

As noted earlier, there is a clearly existing connection between Indian martial traditions and religious practices. With additional investigations of this topic, further information on the practices and aims associated with the overlap of martial-meditative techniques and philosophies will be likely forthcoming, for other Indian martial arts are still in need of systematic investigation.

11

[1] Staal, no date
[2] Draeger and Smith, 1969
[3] Zarrilli, 1989a
[4] Mujumdar, 1950; Savanta, 1914
[5] Egerton, 1968; Mujumdar, 1950; Pant, 1970
[6] Alter, 1992; Fischer, 1963
[7] Deshpande, no date; Rosu, 1981; Staal, 1983–84
[8] see detailed analyses of these relationships in Rosu, 1981; Zarrilli, 1978, 1992a, 1992b, in preparation
[9] Rosu, 1981; Zarrilli, no date b
[10] Zarrilli, 1979, 1984
[11] Sreedharan Nair, 1963; Zarrilli, in press a
[12] Maliszewski, 1987; Zarrilli, no date a
[13] Zarrilli, in press
[14] see Zarrilli, in press a, in press b
[15] see Zarrilli, in press b
[16] Ibid.
[17] Zarrilli, 1989b, in press b
[18] Zarrilli, 1989b, in preparation
[19] Zarrilli, in press b
[20] Leitanthem and Mayanglambam, 1984

CHINA

WHILE THEY have achieved greater recognition than their Indian counterparts, the martial arts of China are similarly poorly understood and inadequately researched. Early fighting forms are known to date back to the Zhou dynasty (1122–255 B.C.) and references to archery, wrestling, and various weaponry appear in literature that predates the Christian era. A close association between ritual dances and the martial arts has led to divergent theories concerning the origins of Chinese combat systems; some speculate that they may have emerged as a category of Daoist physical exercises[1] while others believe that they constituted distinct martial arts that later incorporated Daoist principles within their practices.[2]

Identifying significant personages central to the physical development and philosophical evolution of the martial arts proves even more problematic than the concern for their origins. Nonetheless, though lacking in strong documentation, a persistent belief today credits Bodhidharma (ca. A.D. 448–527) as being a central figure in the development of a systematized martial system. Bodhidharma (Skt.; Chin., Putidamo or Damo; Jpn., Bodai Daruma Daishi) is an obscure figure in the martial arts and Ch'an (Jpn., Zen), as well as in Indian and Chinese history. Several versions regarding details of his life exist.[3] Principal sources of information concerning Bodhidharma's life are derived from *Records of the Transmissions of the Lamp (Jing De Chuan Deng Lu)* compiled by a Ch'an monk, Dao Yuan, in A.D. 1004.[4] The other source is *Biographies of Famous Buddhist Monks (Xu Gaoseng Zhuan)* compiled around A.D. 645 by Dao Xuan.[5] Critical essays including discussions of Bodhidharma have appeared elsewhere.[6] While details remain nebulous, the subject of this writing warrants a discussion of this topic at least in some preliminary fashion.

The earliest records of Buddhism in China date back to approximately the second century B.C. However, it was not until the second century A.D. that Buddhism began to flourish in China.[7] Bodhidharma appeared over two centuries later and is generally acknowledged as the first patriarch of the Ch'an school in China. Although no Indian records of his life are known to exist, other sources indicate that he was the third son of King Sugandha of southern India, a member of the *ksatriya* (warrior) caste who later became an *arhat*. His training in Buddhist meditation took place in Kanchipuram, a province south of Madras. Because of the deathbed wish of his master Prajñatara and the decline of Buddhism outside India, Bodhidharma left for China, first visiting the court of Liang Wu Di at Jiankang (presently Nanjing), later traveling to the realm of Wei in northern China, and finally settling in Luoyang. Bodhidharma also purportedly resided at the Shaolin Temple on Wutai Mountain in Henan Province, although this connection remains speculative as well.[8] Here he is said to have meditated in front of a wall for nine years (*biguan,* Chin., "wall gazing"). At the monastery he observed that many monks were unable to remain awake during meditation. To overcome this problem as well as to improve the health of his disciples, Bodhidharma reportedly introduced a systematized set of exercises to strengthen the mind and body, exercises that purportedly marked the beginning of the Shaolin temple style of boxing. According to legend, these exercise forms were transmitted orally and transcribed by later monks as the *Yijin Jing (Cultivating the Muscles Scripture* or *Sinew Changing Scripture)* and *Xisui Jing (Marrow Cleansing Scripture),*[9] although no verification of Bodhidharma's authorship exists. Some writers[10] have also attributed to Bodhidharma the transmission of a system of exercise known as *Shiba Luohan Shou (Eighteen Hand Movements of the Enlightened One)*. This, too, does not appear to be supported by historical documentation.[11] However, he is often credited with introducing Ch'an Buddhism to the Shaolin Temple. Associations between Buddhism and Chinese martial arts dating back to the sixth century have been documented in the Dunhuang murals.[12]

Bodhidharma was also said to have played a central role in transmitting the *Lankavatara Sutra* (Chin., *Lengjia Jing)* to his disciple Hui Ko, stating that it represented the key to Buddhahood. The *Lankavatara Sutra* is one of nine principal Mahayana texts in Nepalese Buddhism. It occupied an important position in the philosophy of Mahayana Buddhism in China and Japan and existed in China at the time *dhyana* was being introduced. The central thesis of the *Lankavatara Sutra* focused upon the content of enlightenment, including specific reference to such doctrines as mind-only (Skt., *vijñaptimatra* or *cittamatra;* Chin., *rulai cang*) and all-conserving consciousness (Skt., *alayavijñana;* Chin., *alai yeshi* or *cangshi*). To support its thesis, it recorded what was purported to be the Buddha's own inner experience (Skt., *pratyatmagata*) concerning the religious teachings of Mahayana Buddhism. In line with the Ch'an tradition, a central theme of the *Lankavatara Sutra* is the importance placed on a transmission of doctrine from mind to mind rather than basing its faith on the use of words or reliance upon written texts.[13] As time passed, Ch'an teachings eventually became detached from the *Lankavatara*. Instead, attention was turned to the "perfection of wisdom" outlined in tenets of the *Vajracchedikaprajñaparamita Sutra* (Skt.; Chin., *Jingang Boro Jing*) or *Diamond Sutra* (one of the nine Mahayana texts mentioned earlier), largely due to the unsystematic structure and obscurity of the *Lankavatara*.

Buddhist teachings (including those attributed to Bodhidharma) became assimilated in China, permeating such preexisting philosophical-religious concepts as Dao, yin-yang, and the principle of dualism and change,[14] the doctrines of "non-action" *(wu wei)* and "natural spontaneity" *(ziran)*, and the importance placed upon exercises for cultivating internal energy *(lian qi)*[15] and its relationship to the goal of longevity or immortality.[16] The Chinese synthesis of Buddhist and Daoist concepts transformed the previous teachings, the early search for Dao being later replaced by the goal of *jian xing* (to see the Buddha-nature in one's self).[17]

Though again lacking in strong evidence, practitioners of modern martial arts often claim to trace components of their system back to the original Shaolin techniques introduced by Bodhidharma. At the present time, the major styles of *gong-fu* are generally divided into two groups—external *(waijia quanfa)* or hard *(gang)* and internal *(neijia quanfa)* or soft *(ro)*. The external system stresses power strikes, greater use of kicks, hand conditioning, and physical strength. It advocates regulation of breath, generating quick movements, utilizing force in straight lines, and responding to force with force.[18] The internal school stresses not only the importance of Daoist and Buddhist philosophical-experiential principles described earlier, but also emphasizes the importance of vital energy *(qi)*, the will *(yi)*, and internal strength. Paralleling practices observed in Kalarippayattu, practitioners seek to collect, cultivate, and store *qi* in the *dantien* (field of elixir),[19] a region located below the navel, through Daoist deep breathing techniques of *qigong*.[20] The internal schools are considered to be defensive and generally focus on approaches that include the following: emphasis on vulnerable body targets and use of clawing and poking hand blows; execution of circular movements; use of a sweeping action for deflection of oncoming attacks; and upsetting the harmony and balance of an attacker by "going with the blow," exploiting the oncoming force of an attack, and absorbing the impact.[21] Shaolin boxing[22] is subsumed within the external classification while styles classified as internal in nature include Taijiquan, Xingyiquan, Baguazhang, and Liuhebafaquan.[23]

In practical usage, all Chinese systems incorporate both "hard" and "soft" elements in their self-defense strategies and techniques. The distinction made between internal and external styles is relatively recent, dating from the beginning of the Qing dynasty (A.D. 1644–1911).[24] Also, current Shaolin styles may emphasize the use of *qi*.[25] As with the internal-external categorization, it is important to note that there is no record of a unique style of boxing associated with the Shaolin monastery until the establishment of the Qing dynasty. Writings present during the Ming dynasty (A.D. 1368–1644) mention that the monks of this institution were working on boxing techniques that had yet to gain any notoriety comparable to other known martial arts styles of the day. Rather, the fame of the Shaolin monastery likely derived from monks making use of a variety of weapons, including the sword and staff.[26]

In addition, the term *gong-fu* is not a system of boxing but rather a generic term for acquired skill. It can also mean task, work performed,

12

special skills, strength, ability, or time spent. Martial art and wrestling appeared as distinct entities during the Han dynasty (206 B.C.–A.D. 220). Terms used at this time included *wuyi* (martial art), *jiaodi* (wrestling), and *shoubo* (boxing)—more obscure terms for boxing included *bian* and *ka*. During the Jin dynasty (265–316), writings referred to *xiangpu* (sumo-style wrestling). The North/South dynasty period (420–589) is noted for records of martial arts forms and health motifs. During the Ming period (1368–1644), the term *quan* (fist) is used to represent martial arts. The Qing period (1644–1911) is noted for the proliferation of different styles, although no new generic names for martial arts were forthcoming. Literature during the Republican period (1911–49) uses the term *guoshu* (national art). More accurately, the terms for Chinese boxing are *quanfa* and *quanshu*. *Wushu* is the term generally used at the present time for martial arts,[27] though the new government of the People's Republic of China has modified its many forms into a cultural gymnastic sport and performing art and uses the term in this context.[28]

The primary internal styles reflect principles of Chinese philosophy and cosmogony. The major style, Taijiquan (Great Ultimate Boxing), usually consists of smooth, flowing, gentle movements with no hesitation observed between the various postures and combinations being performed. *Shifu* Jou Tsung-Hwa (Fig. 12) is pictured here in an informal pose demonstrating the movements found in Taijiquan known as *danbian* (single whip). Rounded curling gestures are the central bodily movement, consisting of kicks, strikes, and evasive actions. These movements are observed in all five major schools (Chen, Yang, Wu, Hao, and Sun) and are based on philosophical concepts of *Taiji* (Great Ultimate), *Taiji Tu* (Diagram of the Great Ultimate), the *Yijing (Book of Changes)*, *wu xing* (five elements or phases), and the interplay of the cosmic principles, yin and yang.[29]

Xingyiquan (Form of Mind Boxing), a second internal style, consists largely of linear movements and emphasizes the use of vertical strength and the fist. There are five major forms of striking—splitting, crushing, drilling, pounding, and crossing—and a dozen other techniques derived from the characteristics of animals. The five forms of striking are generally practiced separately right and left and then combined into a definite pattern. Here, too, movements are based on the philosophical concepts of *Taiji*, the *Yijing*, and yin-yang.[30]

The art of Baguazhang (Eight Diagrams Palm; also referred to as Baguaquan, or Eight Diagrams Boxing) consists of circular movements and the use of horizontal strength and the open palm. Circling postures are either based upon animal movements or inherent bodily reactions. *Bagua* signifies the eight trigrams of traditional Chinese thought (as derived from the *Yijing*) and have correspondence in one designation to areas of the head and torso and, in another classification, to the limbs of the body. The essence of Baguazhang is its ever-changing circling movement, reflecting the circular diagram composed of the eight trigrams. According to this conceptual scheme, a more complex diagram can be found in which the Primal Arrangement (Sequence of Earlier Heaven) is represented by an inner circle of eight trigrams while the Inner World Arrangement (Sequence of Later Heaven), consisting of an alternative arrangement of the trigrams, surrounds the first circle on the outside.[31] Another theory suggests that actual designation may stem from defensive and attacking movements of practitioners around eight posts representing imaginary opponents. These eight posts were arbitrarily named *bagua*, this being a common symbol for the eight directions (four cardinal, four corners). The name *bagua* symbolizes the fact that Baguazhang is a fluid style that allows one to attack or defend from any direction.

Liuhebafaquan (Six Harmonies and Eight Methods Boxing) is a northern form of *gong-fu* that stresses a continuous flow of arm and hand movements including fingertip strikes, palm strikes, hand-trapping elbow strikes, and wrist locks, though kicks may be directed to an opponent's legs. An example of these movements is found in the technique known as *Zhelong Quan Zhi Quanshou Yongfa* (Hibernating Dragon Method of Circling Hands). This sequence illustrates a defense against a punch to the face (Figs. 13–14). From a "cat stance" position, *Shifu* Wai Lun Choi steps forward with his left leg and blocks the strike with his right hand (Fig. 15), while simultaneously placing his left hand on his opponent's elbow (Fig. 16) and redirects his weight against the opponent (Fig. 17). Torquing his waist, stepping forward with his right leg and initiating a clockwise motion with his right arm all at the same time, Choi finishes the technique by delivering a palm strike to the opponent's groin (Fig. 18).

The major organs of the body (e.g., heart, kidneys, lungs, liver) are each associated with one of the five phases or elements *(wu xing)*, a particular trigram, a quality of yin or yang and one of the five directions (north, south, east, west, center). This is done because a major goal of practice is to improve circulation and harmonize the organs to ensure their proper functioning and, in turn, promote good health.[32]

It is surprising to note that although the internal styles clearly draw upon the principles of Daoist and Ch'an teachings in the use of specific

13

14

15

16

17

18

forms, self-defense techniques, and strategies, there is little emphasis today upon the goals outlined within the classical meditative systems and sought by some of the earlier martial arts practitioners. The importance of health and cultivation of *qi* may still be stressed,[33] but generally remains limited to this aspect of psychophysical development. Meditation in this sense is viewed more as a technique (or self-regulation strategy of cognitive, physical, and psychophysiological activity) useful in achieving psychological well-being and improving physical performance, than a radical psychological transformative process associated with the culmination of a spiritual discipline.[34]

An example of the standing meditative postures associated with the four primary Chinese martial arts is also demonstrated here by *Shifu* Wai Lun Choi: Taijiquan's *mabu zhanzhuang* (horse stance) (Fig. 19); Baguazhang's *wuji zhanzhuang* (infinity posture) (Fig. 20); Xingyiquan's *santishi* (three form style) (Fig. 21); and Liuhobafaquan's *weitogong* (Vedic [posture] exercise) (Fig. 22). A preliminary, common feature of these practices is to relax, breath naturally, empty the mind of all thoughts, and to direct *qi* throughout various parts of the body.

While some writers do describe classical meditative goals as an integral component of internal Chinese martial systems[35] (e.g., experience of the *Dao*, emptiness, the Void, etc.)—these perspectives remain clear exceptions to the teachings stressed in the United States and China today.[36]

19   20

21   22

[1] Needham, 1956
[2] Henning, 1981
[3] see Ch'en, 1964; Draeger and Smith, 1969; Haines, 1995; Masunaga, 1972; Pachow, 1972; Wong, 1978
[4] see Tao-Yuan, 1935
[5] see Tao-Hsuan, 1890
[6] see Maliszewski, 1992c
[7] Chan, 1963
[8] Maliszewski, 1992c
[9] Maliszewski, 1987; Wong, 1978
[10] Chow and Spangler, 1977
[11] see Levi and Chavannes, 1916
[12] see Yi, 1983
[13] Maliszewski, 1987; Wong, 1978
[14] see Lao Tzu, 1963
[15] see Chuang-Tzu, 1968
[16] see Chen, 1973; Yu, 1964–65
[17] Maliszewski, 1987; Wong, 1978
[18] Wong, 1978
[19] see Cheng, 1985b; Huang, 1974; Maspero, 1937/1981a

[20] see Englehardt, 1987
[21] Wong, 1978
[22] Draeger, Kiong, and Chambers, 1976; Draeger and Leong, 1977
[23] see Maliszewski, 1992c
[24] Henning, 1981
[25] Wong, 1978
[26] Henning, 1981
[27] Berk, 1979; Draeger and Smith, 1969
[28] see Mark, 1981; Staples and Chan, 1976
[29] see Maliszewski, 1992c
[30] Liang, 1977; Smith, 1974b
[31] Smith, 1967
[32] see Ch'en, 1969
[33] see Koh, 1981; Maisel, 1974; Mogul, 1980a, 1980b
[34] see Wong, 1979a
[35] see Maliszewski, 1992c
[36] Amos, 1983/1984

KOREA

DUE TO ITS strategic position—China to the west, Manchuria and Russia to the north, and Japan to the southeast—the country of Korea was often beset by warrior factions seeking to control and overtake it. Military contact from Mongolia and China constituted the earliest sources of martial influence in Korea. Early forms of combat known as Subak are reported to have been practiced in the northern regions during the Koguryo dynasty (37 B.C.–A.D. 668).[1]

At the time that Buddhism was being introduced to Korea via China, it had taken on its own unique flavor. In particular, in the kingdom of Silla during the sixth century A.D., social-religious organizations developed, the heads of which were referred to as *hwarang* (Kor., *hwa*, flowers; *rang*, young master; flower boy).[2] Though initially beginning as a social organization for aristocratic youth, this system later evolved into a philosophical code known as *hwarangdo* (Way of the Flower Boy), steeped heavily in Confucian concepts of chivalry and patriotism. Training consisted of education in philosophy, morality, and the arts and sciences, as well as extensive practice of the martial arts, particularly swordsmanship and archery.[3] The four most important historical works containing information on the *hwarang* and *hwarangdo* included the *Samguk Sagi, Samguk Yusa, Hwarang Sagi (Biography of Hwarang)*, and *Xinluo Guoji* (Chin.; Kor. trans., *Sillagukji; History of Silla*). The latter two works did not survive history.[4] There remains no specific documentation of the combat forms used by the Hwarang.[5]

Buddhism was introduced and openly accepted in Silla at this time. Maitreya worship constituted the predominant form of Buddhism. Maitreya (Skt., friendly, benevolent; Chin., Miluofo; Jpn., Miroku; Kor., Miruk; Pali, Metteyya; Tibetan, Byamspa) refers to the next Buddha destined to appear on earth. According to the Korean version of the *Maitreya Incarnation Sutra* (Kor., *Mirukhasaengsongbulgyong;* Chin., *Foshuo Mixia Sheng Shengfo Jing;* Skt., *Maitreya Vyakarana*),[6] the incarnation of Maitreya Bodhisattva (Bodhisattva, Skt., Enlightened being) would appear in Korea after fifty-six thousand million years and attainment of enlightenment would occur under the *Yonghwa* tree. Living beings would be saved and the land would be free from famine, war, pestilence, and other problems. As the interpenetration of Buddhist thought and the *hwarang* ideal grew, a *hwarang* eventually came to be viewed as the incarnation of Maitreya. In time, members of the *hwarang* began calling themselves the men of the *Yonghwa* tree, stating that Maitreya worship formed a bond among them.[7] Indeed, the relationship between the *hwarang* organization and Maitreya was such an intimate one that the formation of a Maitreya cult is suspected.[8]

The *hwarang* spirit consisted of a mixture of Buddhism, Confucianism, Daoism, and Korean primitive religion. Won'gwang, a famous Buddhist priest in Silla, outlined precepts that were adopted by the *hwarang*, which included loyalty to the king, filial piety in regard to parents, sincerity in relations with friends, courage in battle, and selectivity in the killing of living things.[9] The importance of not retreating in battle was perhaps the central tenet adopted by the *hwarang* warrior. To this end, Kim[10] suggests that a parallel between the Buddhist goals adhered to by Won'gwang and the *hwarang* spirit was that battle was one of the means through which the warrior was able to be freed of his ego and ascend to Buddhahood.

Buddhist priests served as advisors to and taught the *hwarang*, and in some cases were actual members of the *hwarang*.[11] The Buddhism in Silla during the sixth century had a strong Mahayana component. However, it did not emphasize meditation and reflection in order to solve life's problems through enlightenment.[12] Rather, it stressed the medium of prayer and its effectiveness in helping the people to fulfill their desires. Buddhism became the state religion in the belief that the state of Silla only could stave off enemy invasions and be protected by the power of Buddha, a belief compatible with the earlier primitive shamanistic Korean religion.[13] Thus, a number of writers have concluded the *hwarang* movement to be essentially shamanistic in nature.[14]

Despite this interesting development, by the late eighth century, the government of Silla began to collapse; the *hwarang* warriors were losing their military effectiveness and eventually turned into disorganized bands of dilettantes.[15] The Koryo dynasty (918–1392) supported Buddhism and a number of martial arts including Subak, Kwonbbop, Yusul, Ssirum, and Gungsul.[16] However, high ideals held by the *hwarang* and intimate association with Buddhism no longer characterized this period. Several systems, such as Subak and Kwonbbop, fell into the category of popular sport or were used more exclusively in military training. In the Yi dynasty that followed (1392–1910), even the interest in these latter two martial arts declined and Confucianism replaced Buddhism as a strong cultural force in Korea. While an open route between Korea and China had existed for the Korean and Chinese martial arts masters prior to the Yi dynasty, Confucian philosophy tended to discourage the practice of the martial systems. With these developments, the arts were kept alive only by the dedication of masters who retreated to remote mountain areas and handed the forms down secretly to select pupils. With the passage of time, even Buddhist philosophy (what remained of it) turned against the practice of the martial arts, the martial role being viewed as contrary to Buddhist philosophical precepts. Following the Japanese takeover of the country in 1894, the educational system of Korea was exposed to the Japanese style of martial sports in the forms of Kendo, Jujutsu, and Judo, while at the same time instruction in military combat techniques was banned. Upon Korea's liberation from Japan in 1945, however, the martial arts again began growing in popularity, though as a sport form (not unlike many of the contemporary *budo* systems of Japan). Included among these disciplines were many of the systems currently seen today, such as Taekwondo, Hapkido, and the like.[17]

The modern martial arts of Korea have little to offer in tracing the historical evolution of martial arts. As has been pointed out elsewhere,[18] with the exception of Taekkyon, few arts actually date back further than fifty or sixty years. Further, while some techniques were imported from China, many were influenced by the Japanese occupation. Even specific techniques of Subak, from which Taekkyon is descended, are unknown. Despite this limitation, it is useful to review several contemporary disciplines that have integrated spiritual components within their conceptual and experiential framework to determine the nature and form of this dimension of practice. Three disciplines to be discussed are Hwarangdo, Kuk Sul, and Simgomdo.

The art of Hwarangdo is a martial system that places strong emphasis upon Chinese philosophical writings in its conceptual foundation, particularly with respect to principles of *um-yang* (Chin., yin-yang) and *ki*. Evolving from *Taeguk* (Kor., Great Ultimate; Chin., *Taiji*), the interaction of the cosmic forces, *um* and *yang*, led to the formation of the five basic elements of matter *(ohaeng)* in the universe: *kum* (gold), *mok* (wood), *su* (water), *hwa* (fire) and *t'o* (earth). The vital energy associated with the dialectical interaction of *um-yang* was *ki* (Chin., *qi*). *Ki* was viewed as the undifferentiated unity of existence and non-existence and the vital force behind life transformation. In conjunction with these

23

principles, this martial art blends principles of hardness and softness and linear and circular motions.[19] On a physical level, Hwarangdo combines hard and soft techniques and integrates circular and linear movements. Self-defense methods include spinning and jumping kicks, hand strikes and blocks, falling and rolling techniques, chokes, joint breaks, and joint manipulation, locks, and throws. As an example of these techniques, *Sahbumnim* Joo Bang Lee demonstrates the movement *yangin ch'orisul*, a defensive technique against two opponents (Fig. 23). Advanced training involves the use of weapons and study of vital points.[20]

Contemporary techniques of this system are founded on four basic divisions of power: inner *(naegong)*, outer *(oegong)*, weapon *(mugigong)*, and mental *(simgong)*. *Naegong* consists of training methods for developing *ki; oegong* relates to external techniques that extend *ki* power outwardly; and *mugigong* consists of techniques in weapon training. *Simgong* is directly concerned with the mental control of *ki* and is divided into thirteen different subdivisions, among which are included putting a person to sleep *(ch'oemyonsul)*, concealing oneself in front of others *(unsinbbop)*, chanting to heal or cause disease *(jusul)*, studying of the laws of the universe *(ohaengbbop)*, and studying the mind *(yusimbbop)*.[21]

24

Development of *ki* is a central theme of Hwarangdo. As an example, *Sahbumnim* Lee demonstrates a sitting mediation technique known as *ki unsinbbop*. This meditation involves emptying the mind of thoughts and directing *ki* throughout the body (Fig. 24). In the human body, this vital force is viewed as concentrating in a region slightly below the navel called *danjon* (red field), which is trisected by three acupuncture points: *kihae* (*ki* ocean), *sokmun* (stone door), and *kwanwon* (first gate). The first point serves as the reservoir of *ki*, the second point is the "keeper of strength," and the third point opens to receive *ki* from the universe. The entire life process is both activated and maintained by *ki*, which is circulated through twenty-six meridians to various parts of the body. Cultivation of *ki*, achieved through exercises of breathing *(danjon hohupbbop)* and mental concentration *(jongsindobbop)*, is the central medium through which shifts in consciousness are viewed as unfolding.[22]

Human consciousness has been viewed within this system as a circle divided into quarters. The first quadrant (clockwise, 0°–90°) encompasses the range of normal human behavior, including activities of physical coordination and strength. Techniques of *ch'oemyonsul* and *unsinbbop* are subsumed within the upper ranges of this quadrant. The second quadrant (90°–180°) covers the range of "extraordinary human powers" and includes clairvoyance, telepathy, and out-of-body experiences. *Jusul, ohaengbbop,* and *yusimbbop* are practices associated with this quadrant. Here also the practice of meditation begins. The third quadrant (180°–270°) covers the range of what are described as "supernatural powers" and is viewed as the realm of the *dosa.* The term *dosa* (Kor.) can refer to a Daoist or an enlightened Buddhist. Within Hwarang-do, this term is equated with "Buddhist high priests." It is at this stage that one traditionally renounced secular life and retreated to mountain regions to engage in further religious practices. Subsumed within this quadrant are activities commonly associated with Korean shamanism, including physical transformations and communication with spirits. (However, such phenomena are not necessarily viewed as part of formal meditative practice.) The final quadrant (270°–360°) is the category of the Buddha in which the physical body is perfectly unified with the universal *ki* and becomes pure spirit or vital force. Completion of activities in the last two quadrants (180°–360°) leads to *dot'ong* (traditional meaning, understanding of *Do* or Way).[23] Despite an important position accorded to advanced meditative practices and goals (third and fourth quadrants) the metaphysical teachings are currently de-emphasized, with physical components being stressed (i.e., those activities falling within the realm of the first two quadrants).

A second Korean martial art that deserves mention is Kuk Sul. Due to the Japanese suppression of Korean martial arts between 1894 and 1945, an attempt was made to systematize the various forms of martial techniques found in Korea. Information was reportedly collected from historical and contemporary sources to organize a single Korean martial art.[24] On a physical level, Kuk Sul consists of kicks, hand strikes, wrist-twisting techniques, locks, and throws. An example is found in the throwing technique known as *jonhwanbbop* as demonstrated here by *Sahbumnim* In Hyuk Suh. This technique is executed as a defense against a single wrist grab whereby the defender initially offsets the opponent's balance forward and then circles the hand down and around forcing the opponent to turn forward and be thrown (Figs. 25–28).

The study of vital points is also a component of this system. Advanced training involves application of basic defense in a seated or prone position as well as the use of weapons including short sticks, staff, sword, double knives, and fan.[25]

The development of *ki* is an integral component of this system, and reference is made to several monks who are described as being instru-

25

26

27

28

mental in developing the philosophy of *ki*. Wonhyo (617–86) reportedly employed techniques of *hwalbbop* and *hyolbbop* (stimulating and neutralizing vital points in the body) to heal individuals suffering from terminal maladies. Sosan (1520–1604) and Samyongdang (1544–1619) later allegedly incorporated these two techniques with *jangsuyangsaengbbop* (the way of taking care of one's health for longevity) and *okwanbbop* (moderation in the use of five senses: hearing, tasting, seeing,

58 SPIRITUAL DIMENSIONS OF THE MARTIAL ARTS

29

smelling, and feeling) to reach *doinbbop* (literally, way of attaining the level of high priests; i.e., *dosa*), a method used to achieve longevity.[26]

At the present time, *ki* is classified into two different types: *sonch'onjok ki* (prenatal or innate *ki*) and *huch'onjok ki* (postnatal *ki*). Three acupuncture points *(umkyo, kihae, sokmun)* descending in a vertical line directly below the navel *(singwol)* represent the area encompassed by the first type of *ki* and three different acupuncture points *(subun, hawan, gurli)* ascending in a vertical line above the navel constitute the postnatal *ki* centers. Prenatal *ki* is fully developed before birth (though it can be weakened through such outside factors as stress) and determines inner strength and power. Postnatal *ki* develops after birth and is the source of external strength. Through meditation *(myongsang)* primarily associated with Son (Chogye order), concentration *(jongsin t'ongil)*, and breathing exercises *(danjon hohupbbop)*, prenatal and postnatal *ki* are combined—initially by stimulating those two acupuncture points nearest the navel *(umkyo* and *subun* respectively) and later applying this same technique to the other points—a process that eventually increases both internal and external power. Symbolically, combining prenatal *ki* and postnatal *ki* also represents the interaction of *um* and *yang* respectively.[27] *Sahbumnim* In Hyuk Suh is found here demonstrating a sitting meditation posture known as *ki son*. With his hand raised, *ki* is channeled into the hand later to be used in martial application (Fig. 29).

While mental and physical training follow a progressive, hierarchical series of stages, the importance accorded *ki* development is evident at the highest level of training where the practitioner receives training in *kiui worli* (principles of *ki*) and *kihak* (study of *ki*). Within *kiui worli*, one studies the physical structure of the human body and its interrelationship with the 364 vital points. With respect to the physical dimension, *kihak* involves studying some 270 original techniques that are broken down and expanded into 3,608 parts. On the meditative side, the practitioner studies principles underlying the interaction of prenatal *ki* and postnatal *ki*, the use of concentration *(jongsin t'ongil)*, and the practice of meditation *(myongsang)*, which ultimately leads to *dot'ong*. However, it is estimated that twenty to thirty years' work is needed to master this specialized training, a factor that clearly limits the number of practitioners of the art.[28]

In contrast to models observed in Hwarangdo and Kuk Sul, there is a Korean martial system that does rely heavily upon the practice of meditation and wherein the role of enlightenment is viewed as central to its teachings and techniques. Having only evolved within the past two decades, the art of Simgomdo (and its sister discipline of Sinbbop) presents an unusual course of development, compatible with the Korean historical-religious tradition yet atypical in the standard evolution of most martial arts. The founder, Chang Sik Kim, originally began formal meditation training in Son at the Hwagye Temple in Seoul, Korea at the age of thirteen. Following the teachings of Son Master Seung Sahn,[29] activities were essentially limited to setting meditation and general work chores performed at the temple. At the age of twenty-one and with no previous martial arts training, Kim attended a one-hundred day meditation retreat at Samgak Mountain and attained enlightenment in the art of Simgomdo in 1965. During the course of this retreat, a series of visions appeared to him, which consisted of hundreds of martial arts forms, which he memorized and later practiced. From this unexpected and initially frightening experience, the art of Simgomdo was developed.[30]

Simgomdo (*sim*, mind; *gom*, sword; *do*, way) is a discipline devoted primarily to the study of the sword. Using a wooden weapon, the student engages in the practice of both mental and physical exercises. Physical exercises consist of learning a series of progressively more difficult forms designed to strengthen and loosen muscles, improve coordination, and enhance speed, timing, and concentration. Mental training consists of chanting *(yombul)*, light breathing exercises *(danjon hohupb-*

bop) (without strong emphasis upon cultivation of *ki*), the use of *kongan* (Kor.; Chin., *gongan;* Jpn., *koan*), active (movement) meditation that focuses upon keeping the mind clear from moment to moment, and sitting meditation. As an example, *Sahbumnim* Chang Sik Kim is found here demonstrating the opening position of a *ch'amson* (sitting *son*) sword form in Simgomdo (Fig. 30). Sitting meditation consists of mental visualization of martial arts forms that can later be applied without effort in physical movement. The unarmed aspect of Kim's teachings is known as *sinbbop* (body technique). Emphasis in training is placed upon practicing basic motions, such as circular hand and foot combinations, that are combined into forms and in later advanced training lead to free-fighting. With its non-intellectual focus, the goal of sword and empty-hand practices is to "cut thinking," a process that leads to enlightenment *(dot'ong)*. Currently this martial art is taught both in Korea and in the United States.[31]

30

Outside of the martial arts mentioned in detail thus far, some of the other present-day Korean martial arts also emphasize Zen or spirituality within their respective disciplines.[32] This influence appears to be more directly adopted from the contemporary Japanese influences described earlier. In keeping with Draeger's[33] observations of contemporary Okinawan and Japanese Karate-do, it is feasible that, for the vast majority of Korean martial arts, the recent import of Zen (and "spirituality") marks the attempt to bring metaphysical principles into an art in support of claims to 1. possess higher ideals than the "mere" physical aspects of the art, or more optimistically, 2. enhance the physical performance of the martial art practitioner through the integration of Zen exercises—similar to the *hwarang* warriors' association with Buddhism noted earlier.

However, before a final evaluation can be made concerning the status of contemporary Korean martial arts with respect to meditative-religious teachings, it should be pointed out that individual exceptions to the current trend delimiting meditative practices may be observed. The writings of Shim, for example, illustrate how a martial art (Taekwondo) generally taught with a primary emphasis upon the physical dimension and moral development can borrow from the meditative/religious disciplines and integrate within it the teachings and goals of the classical meditative systems.[34]

[1] Young, 1993
[2] Tamura, 1974
[3] H. An, 1977; K. An, 1974; Mo, 1978
[4] Kim, 1961, 1965/1966
[5] Young, 1993
[6] see Maliszewski, 1992c
[7] Tamura, 1974
[8] Henthorn, 1971
[9] Ilyon, 1972; Kim, 1931
[10] Kim, 1965/1966
[11] Ibid.
[12] Hatada, 1951; Murayama, 1932
[13] Kim, 1965/1966
[14] Ayukai, 1931, 1932; Mishima, 1934a, 1934b, 1934c; Rutt, 1961; Yang, 1957
[15] Draeger and Smith, 1969; Rutt, 1961
[16] Draeger and Smith, 1969
[17] see Maliszewski, 1992c
[18] see Young, 1993
[19] Lee, 1978
[20] Lee, 1978, 1979, 1980
[21] Lee, 1978
[22] Lee, 1978; Maliszewski, 1992c
[23] Ibid.
[24] see Maliszewski, 1992c
[25] I. S. Suh, 1982; I. H. Suh, 1986
[26] S. S. Suh, no date
[27] Hallander, 1984; Maliszewski, 1992c
[28] Maliszewski, 1992c
[29] see Seung, 1982
[30] Kim and Kim, 1985; Maliszewski, 1992c
[31] Ibid.
[32] Chung, 1979; Son and Clark, 1968
[33] Draeger, 1974b
[34] Shim, 1974, 1980, 1984

JAPAN

MARTIAL TRADITION holds an important position in Japanese culture and history. However, as late as the eighth century, formal, systematic combat methods for training warriors had yet to be formally developed. Four centuries later, however, the classical professional warrior, known as *bushi* (Jpn.), had risen to a politically powerful position, playing a significant role in developing the national character of Japan.[1] This favorable climate permitted the *bushi* to further develop and refine the combative techniques of *bujutsu* (martial arts) in the years that followed. Some sixty different combat systems organized around hundreds of formal martial traditions *(ryu)* were known to exist by the seventeenth century.[2]

Zen Buddhism was introduced to Japan from China during the Kamakura period (1185–1333). Two central figures responsible for this introduction were the Japanese Buddhist priests Eisai (1141–1215) and Dogen (1200–53), who had studied Ch'an in China. Through the efforts of their followers Tokiyori (1227–63) and Tokimune (1251–84), Ch'an (as Zen) was introduced into Japanese life and is often acknowledged to have had a distinct impact upon the life of the samurai, one of many ranks of *bushi*.[3] The integration of martial and spiritual teachings (including Shinto, Confucian, and Zen Buddhist doctrine) led to the development of bushido, the warrior code.[4] Espousing such virtues as justice, courage, loyalty, honor, veracity, benevolence, and politeness, the classical warrior was primarily concerned with experiencing a spiritual awakening by achieving the state of *seishi choetsu*, a frame of mind in which one's thoughts transcended life and death.[5]

With the growing importance and favor given to the warrior class, it is interesting to note that the Edo period (1603–1868) is characterized as an age favored by peace. This is essentially due to the formal founding of the Tokugawa military government commonly known as the *bakufu*.[6] Originating in the late twelfth century, the Tokugawa consisted of the successors of various families who supported a dictatorial and aristocratic form of military government. Under the rule of the Tokugawa,

Japan was cut off from the outside world and people were segregated into rigid social classes. Even the privileged warrior class was subject to Tokugawa policy. Fewer wars were fought, which led to a decline in martial skill. In contrast to past tradition, Tokugawa *bushi* held their class distinction through birthright rather than extensive combat training. To further reduce martial ardor, the military government directed its people's attention (*bushi* and commoner alike) to the grandeur of Japan's past and had *bushi* participate in non-martial activities (e.g., acting, dancing, singing, poetry writing) and conform to a Confucian education. It is this shift in social awareness that led to the development of the *budo* forms.[7] Taking a more pragmatic stance, the Japanese culture took the Confucian interpretation of the *Dao*[8] (Chin., Way)—*Do* in Japanese—and with influences of esoteric Buddhism, Shintoism, and Daoism, modified it so it applied to man in his social relationships and was compatible with Japanese feudal society.[9] The transition from *bujutsu* (*bu*, military [martial] affairs; *jutsu*, art; or *bugei* [*gei*, art]) to *budo* (*do*, way) involved a reorientation away from combat training to cultivation of man's awareness of his spiritual nature. The primary goal of early *budo* was enlightenment, similar to what has been described in Zen teachings, external perfection of (martial) technique giving way to self-mastery via "spiritual forging" *(seishin tanren)*.[10] In the state of the "artless art," the experience of the *Do*, the mind was made "pure" (*makoto*, "stainless mind") and "immovable" (*fudoshin*, "immovable mind"), undisturbed by external nonessentials, even the *Do* was forgotten, the *meijin* (master of the *Do* form) acting with the mind unconscious of itself *(mushin no shin)*. This state of no-mindness has been compared to and equated with *satori* (illumination).[11] The distinction in classification made between *bujutsu* (martial arts) and *budo* (martial ways) is often applied even today.[12]

At this point, it would be appropriate to formally define what some Western writers have called classical *bujutsu* and classical *budo*. Classical *bujutsu* refers to those combat systems developed systematically from the tenth century onward that were designed for battlefield use by the warrior. These systems focused on the optimal development of fighting skills and, concerned with broad combat utility, made use of a wide spectrum of weapons. Among these disciplines were Kenjutsu (sword art), Kyujutsu (archery), Jojutsu (stick art), Bojutsu (staff art), and Iaijutsu (sword-drawing art). Classical *budo* developed from concepts initially identified around the mid-1700s. As noted earlier, these were primarily spiritual disciplines. Hence, in contrast to their *bujutsu* counterparts, they had less of a combative orientation and tended to be more specialized, often confining their effectiveness to a particular weapon or type of combat.[13]

Draeger has further remarked that specific *budo* systems first emerged during the early part of the seventeenth century. All of these earlier disciplines evolved from the *bujutsu:* Kenjutsu (sword art) was transformed into Kendo (sword way); in contrast to the traditional Iaijutsu (sword drawing art), the essence of Iaido (sword drawing technique/way) as a spiritual discipline also emerged.[14] While most of the early *budo ryu* focused on the use of weapons, empty-hand *budo* systems also began to appear.[15] A variety of early *budo* forms continued to evolve until the latter part of the nineteenth century. According to Draeger, with the beginning of the Meiji Era, the aims of what he has called the classical *bujutsu* and classical *budo* systems were redirected by the government to develop a new sense of personal and national spirit, thus leading to the development of the modern disciplines. It should be pointed out that Japanese scholars and practitioners generally do not draw distinctions between classical and modern disciplines. However, for heuristic purposes, this classification, made by some Western writers,[16] can be of assistance in analyzing Japanese martial traditions.

Continuing with the classical-modern distinction, the overthrow of the Tokugawa government in 1868 loosely marks the emergence of modern *bujutsu* and modern *budo*. Differences between these systems and the classical disciplines are described as significant. As a whole, the modern disciplines are generally categorized as methods of self-defense or as tactics for sparring or grappling with an opponent. Many modern *bujutsu* systems consist of officially approved, government-sanctioned methods of hand-to-hand combat that are limited to either practice by law enforcement groups for the purpose of dealing with criminal offenders or use by average citizens as methods of self-defense and spiritual training. While classical *bujutsu* involved battlefield combat, its modern counterpart was applied in civil contexts to restrain assailants rather than to maim them or take their lives.

An illustration of a *jutsu* art is in order. One of the most familiar is Kenjutsu which may be described as an aggressive sword art of Japan. From the ninth to the middle of the seventeenth century, *bushi* used the sword to establish and maintain order in Japan. The sword itself was used with two hands and several hundred different fighting postures *(kamae)* were developed to wield this weapon. Training could involve learning to use the long sword and short sword singly or together. Each

31

32

66 SPIRITUAL DIMENSIONS OF THE MARTIAL ARTS

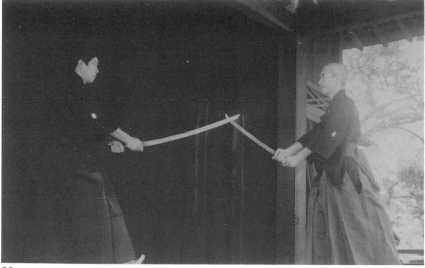

33

of the different *ryu* had different *kamae* and battle tactics. Kenjutsu is believed to have become formally systematized during the Muromachi period (1392–1573).

As illustration of this discipline, Kato *Sensei* (wearing glasses) and Ito *Sensei* of the Kanbe line of Yagyu Shinkage-ryu of Nagoya, Japan, are observed practicing *koden* (old transmission) of Kenjutsu *kata, San Gaku En Itto Ryodan,* using *fukurojinai* (lacquered leather-encased bamboo sticks) (Fig. 31). Notice the lacquered leather *kote* (arm protection) on the *uchidachi* (striker). This is followed by a photograph of Miyauchi Akira *Sensei* of the Kashima Shinden Jiki Shinkage-ryu assuming a *kamae* known as *tenchi* (heaven and earth) prior to engaging an opponent (Fig. 32). This posture, sometimes referred to as *nio-dachi* (the posture of the two temple guards found at the gate of Buddhist temples) indicates the practitioner's determination to be unmoved.

Reflective of the underlying spiritual roots of this tradition is a photograph of swordsman Yoshida Hajime (left) and Namiki Yasushi, 18th headmaster of the Jiki Shinkage-ryu (right), demonstrating *marubashi,* the most advanced level of Kenjutsu of that tradition (Fig. 33). Yamaoka Tetsuo, a swordsman and Meiji statesman, upon seeing Yamada Hachiro perform *marubashi,* noted: "Is there something so profound as this attainable in the way of the sword? If one trains in this, there is no need to practice *zazen!* This is *ritsuzen* (standing or actively moving meditation) which is the true essence of the Zen idea of transmission outside the scriptures . . . a state of union."

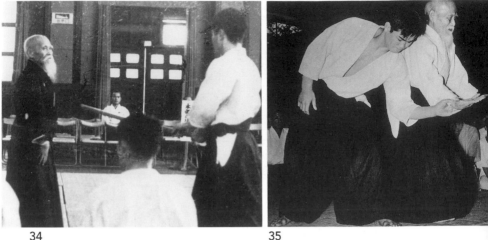

34   35

Modern *budo* systems generally consist of unarmed techniques of grappling or sparring that serve as a means of physical exercise or sport, methods of self-defense, or a form of spiritual training, the goal of which is to bring man into harmony with the values of a peace-seeking international society.[17] Subsumed within the classification of modern *budo* are such disciplines as Aikido, modern Judo, Karate-do, Kendo, modern Kyudo, and (Nippon) Shorinji Kempo.[18] Depicted within the photo illustrations included here are Aikido and Kyudo.

Aikido is primarily an unarmed method of self-defense based on principles of non-resistance to and harmony with one's opponent that makes use of circular movements to gain control of an attacker's momentum, thus neutralizing aggressive actions. It was founded in 1942 by Ueshiba Morihei who had studied Yagyu Kenjutsu, Hozoin Sojutsu and Daito-ryu Aiki Jujutsu earlier. Evolving out of Ueshiba's own physical and spiritual development, this system stresses the importance of mind and body in harmony utilizing physical techniques that largely consisted of throwing and grappling, the latter in the form of joint-locking techniques. There are now many styles of this art, although Ueshiba's emphasis on spiritual aspects distinguishes his "original" form from many other subsequent styles.

A series of photographs are presented here illustrating both physical movements and spiritual practices that comprised this martial art as

36

displayed by its founder, Ueshiba Morihei. In the first picture, he prepares for an armed attack by an opponent and demonstrates *fudoshin* (immovable mind), undisturbed by external distractions (Fig. 34). In the second picture, he is seen near age 80 performing the basic movement known as *tai-no-henko* (posture changing). The technique neutralizes an opponent's attack and culminates with both practitioners facing in the same direction. Here this blending movement is performed with Chiba Kazuo (Fig. 35). In the last picture, Ueshiba is observed seated in prayer in a photograph taken during the early 1960s (Fig. 36). Ueshiba was a follower of practices observed in esoteric Shingon Buddhism and Omoto-kyo, the latter constituting a contemporary Japanese world renewal religion.

Modern Kyudo is a term for Japanese archery. It did not achieve status as a definite *budo* entity until the twentieth century. While younger exponents of this art largely pursue it as a sport form, others seek to develop mastery (unity) of mind, body, and bow. There are several stages involved in shooting the bow that cultivate development of this state of mind. To this end, hitting and penetrating the target takes a secondary position behind self-discipline and spiritual values. A series of photographs are presented here that provide greater detail and insight into the spiritual and mental components that comprise this art.

The first picture is Suhara Koun *Sensei*, Zen priest of Dokuto-an, Engaku-ji, and Kyudo master of the Enma school in Kamakura, Japan. It is rare today to find this combination of being both a Zen priest and Kyudo master. Here he is meditating in order to settle the mind in preparation for the stages of Kyudo that follow (Fig. 37). He is then observed performing a preliminary exercise prior to standing up, setting his stance, and shooting. This is the first stage in Kyudo known as *ashibumi* (to step or thread) (Fig. 38). The third stage is Kyudo is known as *yugamae* (setting the bow). Note the preparedness posture, reflected in both attitude and manner of holding the bow (Fig. 39). *Kai* (meeting), is the sixth and most important stage of Kyudo (Fig. 40). When the bow is extended to its maximum, it encompasses everything, the whole (symbolized by the *enso* circle). Oneness of mind and body, a state of selflessness, must prevail at the moment of execution. The target, bow, and arrow merge to become one with the self. The target is penetrated so there is no longer any need to shoot. This is "to shoot without shooting." At this level of selflessness, *mushin* (natural mind devoid of delusions) prevails and one enters Zen. The last of eight stages *(hassetsu)* used in the process of shooting in Kyudo is known as *zanshin* (remaining heart and mind). While the arrow has been released, at this stage the mind must always be alert and never dwell on the end (Fig. 41).

37

38

39

40

41

42

Centers can be found in different parts of the world that provide training of a spiritual orientation in this more esoteric martial art. One such location is Chozen-ji, International Zen dojo of Hawaii shown in the following two photographs. The first photograph illustrates the target *(mato)* observed at Chozen-ji Kyudo dojo (Fig. 42). The target can be the enemy, the symbol of one's ego, or enlightenment. When the ego is dominant, external preoccupation with achievement and performance (hitting the target) reduces one's proficiency in the art. When one is able to quietly perceive one's breath and faithfully observe one's form (posture or attitude of the mind and body), the arrow becomes an extension of the soul and as such is the "living arrow." The target acts as a gauge to the effect of the arrow penetration: a "living arrow" penetrates the target smoothly and deeply whereas a "dead arrow" merely makes contact with the surface. The second photograph shows Kyudo trainees in *zazen* (Fig. 43). *Zazen* is a prerequisite to all *budo* training at Chozen-ji, affording the trainee a better insight and flow into the active meditation of *budo*. Note the hand position *(hokkai-join):* an alternative hand position is used that is more suitable for *budo* in a dojo and that parallels the stronger breathing process. The calligraphy written above the practitioners reads (from right to left): *mu* (void), *shin* (truth), and *Butsu* (Buddha).

When the modern *budo* are carefully compared to the classical *budo* disciplines, significant differences in orientation can be found. While all *budo* systems address the importance of discipline, moral patterns of behavior, and "spirit," the concept of *Do* in the more contemporary disciplines is given a different emphasis. Redefining this concept in a fashion that subjectively reinforces their own personal needs and role in the world, modern exponents largely overlook the importance placed on radical psychological authentication or transformation of the practitioner. The ethical teachings stemming from Confucian and Daoist writings that stressed the ascetic and moral conduct of the classical warrior have been relegated to the position of romantic literature, subordinate to a "national spirit." This is aptly portrayed in a description found in Draeger:

> To comply with . . . [one's] natural dispositions is called the Way . . . Since the True Way is as facile a matter at this, one should stop acting like a sage, and completely abandon the so-called mind, or the way of enlightenment, and all that is affected and Buddhaish. Let us, instead, not distort or forget this Yamato-gokoro [spirit of Japan], but train and regulate it so that we may polish it up into a straight, just, pure, and good spirit of Japan.[19]

43

And further, a watered-down version of Buddhist philosophy also follows:

> Buddhism has always had much more significance as the "business of state" in Japan than it has had as a religion for individual Japanese. Therefore, Buddhism influences modern *budo* only insofar as it is useful for the realization of absolute truth within secular life. The recognition given by modern exponents to the sacredness of physical effort is a dominant feature in any sense of religion they may possess. Thus, if an exponent puts his whole heart and soul into his training, he is practicing "good Buddhism."

This purported disparity between classical *budo* and modern *budo* is not altogether new in Japanese thought. A similar distinction could also be noted in the effect that Zen had upon classical *bujutsu*. In general, the *bushi* borrowed those aspects of Zen that would improve his abilities and efficiencies as a warrior.[20] To this end, some writers have legitimately questioned the impact, if any, that Zen had upon the warrior's system of ethics,[21] or as a class, if they actually relied upon it.[22] Other exponents who lean toward the broader, less confined version of *budo* believe Zen clearly did effect changes in practitioners and their respective disciplines.[23]

Similarly, both the older *budo* and *bujutsu* traditions often had a close association to Shintoism or esoteric Buddhist doctrines *(mikkyo)* derived from Shingon and Tendai sects.[24] Those warriors adhering to the Buddhist practices often made use of such esoteric devices as *mandara* (Skt., *mandala*), *jumon* (Skt., mantra), *ketsu-in* (Skt. *mudra*), and various ritual implements as a means of achieving protection in battle.[25] Even within classical and modern *bujutsu*, esoteric religious practices existed.[26] As illustration, note a typical *kami-dana* (Shinto shrine) found in the training halls of all Japanese classical martial traditions (Fig. 44). Trainees show respect to their shrine by bowing to it upon entering and leaving the hall at the beginning and end of training sessions.

However, it would be premature to conclude that all of the contemporary *budo* systems that exist today represent empty shells of once-thriving, authentic spiritual disciplines. For example, select schools of modern Kendo and Kyudo do stress the importance of radical psychological authentication or transformation of the practitioner.[27] As further examples, the respective founders of Aikido, Ueshiba Morihei, and the Karate-do style of Kyokushin, Oyama Masutatsu, as well as the succes-

深名神道夢想深杖道

深祖夢想権之助勝吉

44

sor of the Goju-ryu in mainland Japan, Yamaguchi Gogen, have each demonstrated the effectiveness of their respective systems and their use as a medium of effecting personal enlightenment in Draeger's "classical" *(Do)* sense of the word.[28] To this end, an assessment of the individual practitioner within a particular discipline remains the best measure of the degree to which these specific budo aims are stressed, exemplified, and realized. Indeed, taking Ueshiba's martial way of Aikido as an example, many variants of the original style have appeared in the natural evolution of this modern *budo* form as the system itself initially evolved from Daito-ryu Aiki Jujutsu, as noted earlier. Some of these newer forms in fact de-emphasize the spiritual *budo* tenets that Ueshiba adhered to and which made his personal approach unique. It is also important to note that the older budo disciplines are still practiced today in Japan, though commitment to these martial ways involves a level of dedication, perseverance, and discipline seldom observed in contemporary society.[29]

One final martial tradition deserves attention here, though it does not fall clearly within the *bujutsu/budo* delineation. Ninjutsu, the art of martial espionage or "stealing in" (*nin*, 1. stealth, secretiveness; 2. endurance, perseverance; derived from the word *shinobi*, referring to the earliest forms of Ninjutsu; *jutsu*, art) is generally believed to have originated in Japan during the reign of Empress Suiko (A.D. 593–628). Its earliest beginnings date back to the ancient Chinese text on military science called *Sun Tzu Ping Fa* (Chin.; *The Art of War*) written by the

Chinese strategist Sun Wu (also known as Sun Tzu and Sun Zi) who had lived sometime between 500 and 300 B.C.[30] According to legend, monks and shamans had come from China to dwell in forests and caves of the Kii Peninsula with the already present Japanese *yamabushi, sennin, gyoja,* and *shugenja,* bringing with them a knowledge of Chinese military tactics and mystical teachings. A number of Chinese mystic priests such as Kain *Doshi,* Gamon *Doshi,* and Kasumigakure *Doshi* were purported to have taught these early ninja forerunners many of the esoteric ways that later appeared in the doctrines of esoteric Japanese Buddhism.[31] Depicted here is a statue of the scholar monk Kukai (Fig. 45), posthumously known by the name Kobo Daishi, who, along with the monk Saicho, is generally credited with the introduction of the esoteric *mikkyo* (secret doctrines) to Japan in the early 800s.

Ninjutsu attained its greatest notoriety during the Kamakura era. At this time, a number of individuals became disassociated from the court or *bushi* ranks of mainstream Japanese society, many seeking refuge with the warrior-mystics in the Iga or Koga areas of south-central Japan. They settled down in the wild mountainous regions, the natural inaccessibility of which allowed them to develop the martial techniques of their early predecessors to a very high degree of specialization. Concurrent with these developments, various *bushi* would hire *ninja* to engage in espionage for them. *Ninja* were not of the aristocratic *bushi* class, but relegated to a low social strata known as *hinin* ("nonhuman," a social outcast). The daring deeds and exploits of these practitioners had little parallel in the annals of martial espionage,[32] though fictionalized accounts persist to this day.

Traditionally, physical and practical training in Ninjutsu involved developing skills in both armed and unarmed combat. Weapon training included the use of the sword, spear or lance fighting, throwing blades, as well as fire and explosives. Unarmed self-defense methods consisted of: 1. techniques for attacking the bones—strikes, punches, kicks, and blocks directed toward the attacker's skeleton; 2. grappling techniques—locks, throws, and chokes directed against joints and muscles of an adversary; and 3. assorted complementary techniques including tumbling and breaking falls, leaping and climbing, as well as special ways of running and walking. Techniques of this variety are taught by modern-day proponents of Togakure-ryu Ninjutsu,[33] although it should be pointed out that tracing the present-day martial art of Ninjutsu to its earliest forms is a difficult task.

Modern accounts, however, seldom address the spiritual elements

45

associated with Ninjutsu. To begin, practitioners of Togakure-ryu Ninjutsu prefer to refer to their art as Ninpo (*nin*, 1. stealth, secretiveness;
2. endurance, perseverance; *po*, law; *ninpo*, universal law as applied
through the consciousness of persevering). Reportedly drawing upon
the Tantric tradition of Sino-Japanese esoteric Buddhism, the doctrine
of Ninpo Mikkyo (secret knowledge or teaching) taught that all physical aspects of existence originated from a common source and could be
classified in one of five elemental manifestations of physical matter: *chi*
(earth), *sui* (water), *ka* (fire), *fu* (wind), and *ku* (emptiness). Studying
the interrelationship of these principles, the *ninja* applied them in physical combat situations to gain insight into the nature of the universe. The
use of *mandara, jumon,* and *ketsu-in* as well as other esoteric practices
such as energy channeling *(kuji-in)* and balancing electromagnetic power
fields *(kuji-kiri)* were also used to further the practitioner's understanding of the material and spiritual aspects of the universe, the balancing of
these two realms being viewed as necessary in the way to enlightenment.[34]

46

Several photographs are presented here that serve to illustrate the spiritual aspects of this tradition. The *kongokai mandara* is a graphic symbolic representation of the spiritual realm, the "god's eye view of the universe" (Fig. 46). The *taizokai mandara* constitutes a graphic symbolic representation of the material realm, the "being's eye-view of the universe" (Fig. 47). Also displaying esoteric spiritual roots here is the *kamiza* (spiritual seat) at the central point of *Shidoshi* Stephen K. Hayes' personal training hall (Fig. 48). The shelf is flanked by portraits of Grandmaster Hatsumi Masaaki and his teacher Takamatsu Toshitsugu. Artwork and calligraphy by the grandmaster symbolize the tradition behind the art, and the miniature shrine in the center houses a small mirror to remind practitioners in the dojo of the depth of the void or "formless potential" realm. *Shidoshi* Hayes demonstrates the Ninpo Mikkyo *ketsu-*

47

48

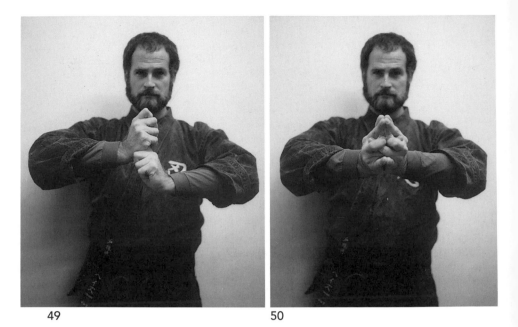

49   50

in hand posturing for the *rin* attitude of godlike strength in the face of mental or physical trial (Fig. 49); the *sha* attitude of health-generating energy channeling from the *kuji-no-ho* series of nine body, will, and mind-protection combinations (Fig. 50); and *retsu,* which is used for the facilitating of clairvoyant knowledge that penetrates through the limits of time and space (Fig. 51).

Aside from employing the theory of five elements *(gogyo setsu)* in conjunction with self-defense techniques, other disciplines were subsumed within the training repertoire, including: the study of Chinese principles *(on'yodo;* Chin., yin-yang); meditation *(meiso)* and concepts of mysticism *(shinpi);* the use of the *Ekikyo* (Chin., *Yijing*); and the development of personal clarity *(seishin-teki kyoyo).* However, these aspects of Ninpo training were more philosophical and practical, rather than geared directly to the realization of personal enlightenment. Meditative exercises that were directed to the goal of radical, psychological authentication or transformation consisted largely of methods of breathing and concentration imported from China. With the impact of Japanese culture, the primary focus came to be directed to the experience of *satori.*

Comparing the secret teachings *(mikkyo)* of Togakure-ryu Ninpo to those of the Shingon and Tendai sects of Japanese Buddhism reveals

51

many similarities. However, the interest displayed by ninja in this area was devoid of the rituals and religious-philosophical premises that characterized the Buddhist sects. Further, the degree to which practitioners of the art of Ninpo met the spiritual goals depends largely on the period in history in which the movement is analyzed: those early collections of family clans that developed Ninjutsu in the late sixth century to the early seventh century A.D. were more directly influenced by the spiritual teachings derived from early Chinese influences, whereas ninja of the 1600s were most likely concerned with military activity and espionage. Today, spiritual goals are stressed in the teachings of several *ryu* (Togakure-ryu Ninpo, Gyokko-ryu Koshijutsu, Kuki Shinden-ryu Happo Hikenjutsu, Gyokushin-ryu Ninpo, Shinden Fudo-ryu Dakentaijutsu, Koto-ryu Koppo Taijutsu, Gikan-ryu Koppojutsu, Takogi Yoshinryu Jutaijutsu, Komogakure-ryu Ninpo) that continue to be practiced in Japan,[35] Europe, and the United States.[36] However, various levels of practice exist, and the degree to which the spiritual dimension is emphasized and actualized will vary from one practitioner to another.

Note: The quoted selections from *Modern Bujutsu and Budo: The Martial Arts and Ways of Japan* are courtesy of Weatherhill Inc.

[1] see Farris, 1993; Friday, 1992
[2] Dann, 1978; Draeger, 1973a
[3] Maliszewski, 1987
[4] Ackroyd, 1987; Hurst, 1990; Kondo, 1978
[5] see Nitobe, 1969
[6] Mass and Hauser, 1985
[7] Draeger, 1973b
[8] Ibid.
[9] Dann, 1978
[10] Draeger, 1973b, 1974a; Maliszewski, 1987
[11] Draeger, 1973b; Suzuki, 1959
[12] Dann, 1978; Draeger, 1973a, 1973b; Uzawa, 1990
[13] Draeger, 1973a, 1973b, 1974b
[14] see Warner and Draeger 1982
[15] see Draeger, 1973b
[16] such as Draeger, 1974
[17] Draeger, 1974b
[18] see Maliszewski, 1992c
[19] Draeger, 1974b, p. 63
[20] Draeger and Smith, 1969; King, 1992
[21] Harrison, 1966; Stacton, 1958; Suzuki, 1959
[22] Collcutt, 1981
[23] Maliszewski, 1992c
[24] Dann, 1978; Lineberger, 1988
[25] see Hall, 1979a, 1979b; Kiyota, 1990
[26] see Maliszewski, 1992c
[27] Ibid.
[28] see Oyama, 1979; Uyeshiba, 1968, 1974; Yamaguchi, 1966
[29] see Maliszewski, 1992c
[30] Sun Tzu, 1963; Tang, 1969
[31] Hayes, 1981b
[32] see Maliszewski, 1992c
[33] Hatsumi, 1981b; Hayes, 1980, 1985
[34] Hayes, 1981a
[35] Hatsumi, 1981b
[36] Hayes, 1980, 1981a

INDONESIA

CONSISTING OF some three thousand islands, Indonesia remains one of the richest centers of ethnic and cultural diversity today. Though little is accurately known of its ancient history, the impact of both cultural and combative influences from other countries such as China, India, and Indochina has been widely documented.[1] Today, Java constitutes not only the cultural and political core of this archipelago, but also remains a center of mysticism and magical-mystical practices, movements that have expanded since independence from the Dutch in 1949.[2] Migrations between peoples of these many islands have been frequent and of long duration, and the combative and mystical elements that continued to evolve over time developed into highly sophisticated martial arts.

Three major combative forms are presently found in Indonesia: Pencak-Silat,[3] Kuntao,[4] and a variety of "endemic" forms.[5] It is generally conceded that Pencak-Silat is the best known self-defense discipline and the one that has the strongest association with spiritual practices. Many theories abound concerning its origins. However, a commonly held view suggests that it first developed in the Minangkabau kingdom on the west central coast of Sumatra. While probably a relatively crude form during its formative development in the eleventh century A.D., by the fourteenth century it had become a highly refined and sophisticated technical art that belonged exclusively to the Madjapahit sultans and their court officials. Over time, the practice of this combative art was open to other social classes. Combative influences derived from Indian, Chinese, and Arabic sources as well as travel among the various islands led to rapid diversification of varying styles currently exceeding over 150 in number.[6]

Combatively speaking, the term *pencak* (Ind.) generally connotes skillful body movements in variation for self-defense, while *silat* (Ind.) refers to the fighting application of *pencak*. While these two components can be demonstrated separately, neither can be said to exist authentically without the other. One of the most eclectic martial arts,

52

53

Pencak-Silat styles make use of both armed and unarmed techniques, employing fast, deceptive movements, blending with an opponent's force and directing it along specific channels where it may then be controlled. Weaponry includes numerous blade, staff, stick, and projective instruments, as well as unarmed techniques that include hand strikes, kicks, grappling, and methods of falling. Technical characteristics of the respective style are determined by physical abilities and cultural mannerisms of the people of a particular area, and major characteristics can be generally localized to specific regions as follows: foot and leg tactics (Sumatra), hand and arm tactics (West Java, Borneo, Celebes), grap-

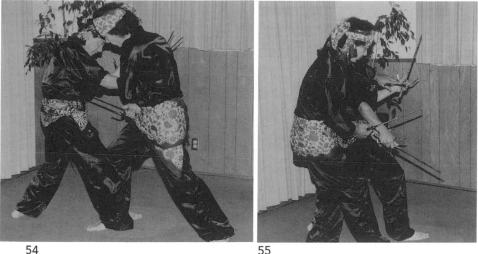

54   55

pling tactics (East Java, Bali, Sumatra), and a synthesis of foot and hand
tactics (Central Java, East Java, Madura, Bali).[7]

An illustration of armed techniques found in Pencak-Silat are depicted here by *Pendekar* John DeJong, a master of the Sumatran Pukulan Sernang style. He is shown here with the *tjabang* (Jav.; *sai*, Jpn.)
performing fundamental movements *(jurus)*. Here, the opponent (left)
attacks DeJong with both *tjabang* at the same time (Fig. 52). DeJong
blocks the weapon on the left with the weapon in his right hand, his left
weapon "sticking" to the opponent's right hand weapon as he moves to
his left (Fig. 53). His right arm then comes under and blocks the opponent's right arm by the elbow with the *tjabang*. He then jabs the right
tjabang into the opponent's stomach (Fig. 54). Pivoting again, the opponent's right arm is blocked by the weapon. The left hand comes in
front, and turning the end of the weapon so that it faces his own elbow,
DeJong hits the opponent on the jaw with both his elbow and *tjabang*
(Fig. 55).

As a formal tradition, spiritual components of Pencak-Silat are
known to have developed through contact with Hindu and Islamic religious teachings. According to tradition, styles of Pencak-Silat take much
from the studies of priests *(pendeta)* who used to study animal movements. The combination of animal actions with various meditative postures employed in religious practices provided the priests with the
necessary skills to protect themselves.[8] Spiritual influences in this part
of the world are also derived from Tantric and Sufi traditions.[9] How-

56

ever, styles will vary as to the degree to which spiritual elements are stressed.

Most systems begin with physical training, learning various movements and applying various techniques to avoid physical injury at the hands of an assailant. Having mastered this preliminary foundation, the practitioner may proceed to develop his inner power, which is expressed in various ways. As examples, within the Silat Setia Hati Terate style of central Java one reportedly employs "hypnosis" to alter an opponent's movements, and the practitioner of the Joduk style of Bali is able to enter a mystic, trance-like state that distinguishes the individual as a *guru* (Ind.; Jav., teacher). An example of this is found in the *kris* dance of western Bali. Supernatural powers are attributed to the *kris* (double-edged daggers), connected with the character of the owner. Villagers performing the dance enter a trance state and reportedly experience no harm even by self-inflicted stabbing movements. Such pre-combat practices are observed in the Joduk style of Pencak-Silat (Fig. 56).

The designation of *maha guru* (master teacher) can be applied to those who engage even further in internal development within the various styles of Pencak-Silat. Finally, those few practitioners who achieve full mastery of their style may be given the title of *pendekar* (Ind.; *pendekar*, Malay, fighter; *pandekar*, Old Jav., skilled duelist) a term that also connotes spiritualist and leader or champion who has obtained an understanding of true (inner) knowledge (believed to be derived from a Menangkabau [Sumatran] expression, *pandai akal,* literally, ability and mind [ability in the sense of complete feeling combined with mind]; or *andeka,* derived from *adhika,* Skt., more, surpassing in quality, integrated into Malay, here referring to a kind of supernatural power possessed by chiefs).[10]

The use of deep breathing techniques (*menarik napas dalam,* Ind.) is central to attaining spiritual capacities and insight. Capabilities reported by practitioners of these techniques include mystic healing, mind reading, precognition, the ability to disable an opponent by touch, identification with and emulation of the characteristics of certain animals, the ability to place spells on enemies, combat invulnerability, and even the power to "kill at a distance."[11] Warrior skills are also closely tied with the possession of power objects (Ind., *jimat;* Jav., *pusaka*), gemstones, carriages, birds, or *kris*. Whatever the object, its power *(kasekten)* is attributed to the infusion of living spirit within it.[12] However, a strict ethical code underlies all defensive and offensive actions.[13] Moreover, the spiritualistic element takes precedence over physical technique, the *pendekar* humbly acknowledging that the real Pencak-Silat is beyond all practitioners of the art.[14]

An illustration of the spiritual elements found within Pukulan Silat Serak can be found in its introductory salutation. The following series of seven photos *Pendekar* Paul de Thouars demonstrates the ritual known as *sembah,* a ceremony performed as part of the introduction to training in this system. It conveys the spiritual purpose underlying the art and is performed prior to engagement in the physical aspects of combat. The following prayer is recited along with the coinciding movements:

> I present myself to the Creator (Fig. 57);
> From the beginning,
> I represent myself to the best of my abilities (Fig. 58);
> I ask to receive from the Creator (Fig. 59);
> in the knowledge of the art (Fig. 60);
> the things that I do not see (Fig. 61);
> to engrave on my heart (Fig. 62);
> until the end (Fig. 63).

The final stage of training in Pencak-Silat is referred to as *kebatinan* (arabic, integrated into Ind., Jav.: *batin,* Ind., inner, internal, in the heart, hidden and mysterious; *kebatinan,* Ind., science of the *batin*). It is im-

57

58

59

60

61

62

63

64

portant to note that Indonesian mysticism (and in particular Javanese mysticism) generally lacks a systematic theology,[15] since the practice of mysticism remains an individual endeavor with great importance placed upon one's own personal revelation and inner emotional experience. For this reason, there are neither dogma nor commonly accepted written sources in Javanese religion.[16] Hence, like the various styles of Pencak-Silat, pursuit of the mystical path incorporates methods and practices that will be different for each sect.

One example of this principle is depicted here in the Batu Mandi style of Pencak Silat of West Sumatra (Fig. 64). It is said that the techniques of Batu Mandi were received by its founder through dreams. This is a variety of *silat gaib* in which techniques are learned through the medium of dreaming. This outdoor training at night may also represent the final test that a student must pass to become a *pendekar*.

Another example is found in the meditation practices of the Sumatran Pukulan Sernang style of Pencak-Silat (Fig. 65). Here the candle serves as an object of concentration. Meditation is used to clear the mind of extraneous thoughts as well as to visualize prospective movements to be performed in practice or actual combat.

Philosophically and experientially speaking, non-martial methods of spiritual development resemble the path of Pencak-Silat in many ways, such as the completion of a series of stages on the mystical path, moving from external concerns in the world to inner development, the impor-

65

tance given to the role of *guru,* and the significance attributed to moral and ethical conduct.[17] The path of *kebatinan* seeks to develop inner tranquillity and the *rasa* (intuitive inner feeling) through a method known as *sujud* (self-surrender). By ridding oneself of bodily desires and other impulses through this self-surrender, one may experience intuitively the divine presence of "God" residing within the heart *(batin).* From another perspective, the inner man is conceived of as a microcosm *(jagat cilik)* of the macrocosm *(jagat gede)* that is Life. The practitioner of *kebatinan* seeks to cultivate the true self *(ingsun sejati),* achieving harmony and ultimately unity with this all-encompassing principle *(manunggaling kawula-gusti)* as well as with his origin and his destination *(sangkan paran).* In this final process, the adept becomes one with ultimate reality.[18]

While the conceptualizations may appear simplistic, the path of *kebatinan* is quite strenuous. One must overcome one's attachment to the outward aspects of existence *(lahir)* through pursuit of such ascetic practices (Jav., *tapa*) as sexual abstinence, fasting, prayer, meditation (particularly visual-concentrative techniques), remaining awake throughout the night, *kungkum* (sitting for hours immersed in rivers during the night at auspicious places), or retreating to mountains and into caves. The purification achieved through *tapa* may lead to *semadi,* a state of mind that, in this cultural context, is best described as world-detached concentration in which one is open to receive divine guidance, knowledge, and ultimately the revelation of the mystery of life, origin, and destiny.[19] Only advanced practitioners make clear distinctions between *tapa* and *semadi.*[20] In non-martial writings concerned with such mystical practices, several types of *semadi* meditation have been distinguished on the basis of their purported goals, thus illustrating a wide range of mystical possibilities. *Semadi* meditation may be practiced to 1. achieve a destructive aim by means of magic, 2. attain a specific positive goal for which greatly enhanced power is needed, 3. experience revelation of the mystery of existence, or 4. achieve ultimate deliverance from all earthly desires.[21] The martial influence of the first goal is clear, though its practice is relegated to a level of "black magic."[22] The third and fourth goals, in contrast, constitute the very purpose of mysticism.

While this conceptual framework may prove useful in conveying the distinct cultural imprint associated with mystical-religious practices in this part of the world, it more than likely detracts from providing a clear picture of the unique and variable forms that the spiritual practices take among various practitioners of Pencak-Silat. It may be misleading to seek specific terms, key words, and concepts of Pencak-Silat as they relate to *kebatinan* insofar as it is unlikely that any two practitioners would hold the same view. Rather, descriptions of specific cases would provide more accurate accounts of what is encompassed within the esoteric practices. Hence, in some circles, use of Indic Javanese terms has diminished, e.g., the Indic Javanese word *semadi* has been replaced by other words such as *sujud* (surrender) and *panembah* (prayer). As noted earlier in regard to other martial arts, the degree to which the mystical practices are pursued and realized will vary from one practitioner to another. Indeed, some *pendekar* today avoid all involvement with magical mysticism and *kebatinan,* while others reportedly test their prowess by practicing the non-corporeal, mystical aspects of their style.[23]

---

[1] Draeger, 1972
[2] Mulder, 1983
[3] Alexander, Chambers, and Draeger, 1970; Cordes, 1990; Koesnoen, 1963
[4] Draeger, 1972
[5] Ibid.
[6] Chambers and Draeger, 1978; Draeger, 1972; Draeger and Smith, 1969
[7] Draeger, 1972; Draeger and Smith, 1969
[8] Draeger, 1972
[9] Stange, 1980/1981
[10] Bisio, 1983; Chambers and Draeger, 1978; Draeger, 1972; Maliszewski, 1987

[11] Draeger, 1972; Draeger and Smith, 1969; Jones, 1983
[12] Stange, 1980/1981
[13] Chambers and Draeger, 1978
[14] Draeger and Smith, 1969
[15] Mulder, 1983; Stange, 1980/1981
[16] Mulder, 1970
[17] Mulder, 1983
[18] Mulder, 1970, 1982
[19] Moertono, 1968
[20] Maliszewski, 1987; Mulder, 1983
[21] Mangkunagara VII of Surakarta, 1957
[22] Mulder, 1983
[23] Maliszewski, 1987

PHILIPPINES

IT IS ONLY within the past twenty years that Filipino martial arts have become generally known among practitioners in the West. Historically, their combat skills were derived from many sources. It is generally thought that an early pygmy tribe called the Negritos were the first settlers to arrive from Central Asia.[1] Three separate Malay migrations followed, beginning around 200 B.C., the last continuing until the middle of the fifteenth century A.D. During this period, the second group of people, called Brahins, came from India to Sumatra, creating the famous Hindu-Malayan empire of Sri Vishaya.[2] The third migration involved the takeover of the Sri Vishayan Empire by the Madjapahit Empire, originally formed in Java.[3] Other than the use of bladed weapons brought by the Malay migrations, martial skills from China entered the country (following earlier Indian influences), promoted by extensive trade relations that had begun in the ninth century. The invasion of these islands by the Spanish conquistadors in the early part of the sixteenth century eventually forced the highly developed martial arts of Kali underground. However, the initial defeat of Magellan at the hands of Lapulapu on Mactan Island served to illustrate the skill of the natives in the use of the blade and hardwood stick as viable weapons.[4]

The martial art of Kali (Tag.; derived from *kalis*, Tag., sabre, sword) came to signify various systems of self-defense that made use of bladed weapons. Dating back prior to the arrival of Portuguese and Spanish explorers in the early sixteenth century, Kali also referred to a stick, empty-hand, or multi-weaponed art that had been used effectively as a system of self-defense by the islanders for centuries.[5]

When the Spaniards returned after their initial defeat, they brought firearms as well as additional reinforcements. Adopting the strategy of conquering specific regions of the islands and then using these natives to conquer their neighbors in adjoining areas, the Spanish victory was assured. Though the Filipino martial arts were outlawed, in 1637 Spanish friars introduced the *komedya* (Tag.; derived from *comedia*, Span.), a socio-religious play that dramatized the religious victory of the Span-

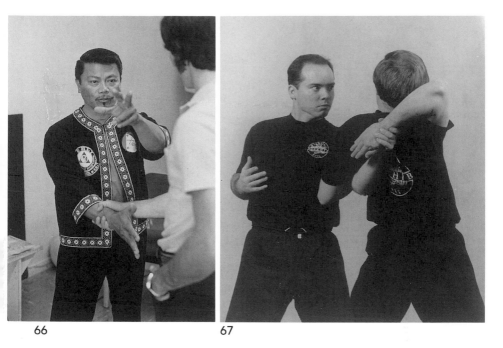

66   67

iards over the natives. This was interpreted as demonstrating the superiority of the Roman Catholic Church over the Muslim faith, the latter being particularly strong in the southern regions.[6] The mock combat portrayed in these plays served to secretly preserve the martial movements and techniques as well as transform aspects of the martial arts that were later outlawed in 1764.[7] These modifications later became known as Arnis (Tag.; derived from *arnes*, Span., harness, decorative trappings; used by the stage actors) and Eskrima (Tag.; derived from *esgrima*, Span., art of fencing).[8] Under American rule in the 1900s, the arts resurfaced and were used to fight the Japanese in World War II. A number of practitioners remained on the islands while others migrated to the United States, settling predominantly in Hawaii and California.

Though its beginnings are rooted in weapons combat—specifically blade, dagger, or stick—the Filipino arts are complete self-defense disciplines, making use of a variety of weapons and empty-hand techniques. Examples of these arts are noted in the next three photographs. First, *Tuhan* Ben Largusa is seen here demonstrating an unarmed defense found in the Largusa-Villabrille Kali system (Fig. 66). Next, Master Mark Wiley (left) performs an empty-hand lock-and-control maneuver found in Biñas Arnis (Fig. 67). Finally, revealing underlying religious

68

overtones, is an interesting picture of Grandmaster Angel Cabales, founder of the Cabales Serrada Escrima system (Fig. 68). Here he displays the posture assumed in issuing a death match challenge *(patayan)*, a practice which existed until 1945. This posture is known as heaven and earth. It signifies the participants' willingness to accept the combative outcome, placing it in God's hands which person will die and go to heaven and which will remain alive on earth.

There are over one hundred styles or systems and they are often divided into three main groups: northern, central, and southern Filipino systems.[9] Generally speaking, northern systems are based on the long stick and long blade, are designed to be used at a long range, and seldom have an empty-hand component. The central systems are based on the principles of sword and dagger (Span., *espada y daga*), use the stick for training and fighting, are designed to be employed at medium range, and have a sophisticated empty-hand art to be used against armed opponents. Finally, southern systems use the blade for training and combat, possess an empty-hand component, and are used at medium or close range. Arnis is the term that refers to those systems generally based on *espada y daga*, while Eskrima often pertains to those systems based on the use of the single stick (*solo baston*, Span., imperfectly acquired, assimilated into Tagalog) or double stick (*double baston* or *doble baston*, Span., also imperfectly acquired and assimilated into Tagalog). Both terms now are largely interchangeable and generally maintain all three components. Terminology is often fluid and imprecise among various practitioners of even the same system.[10]

Unlike other cultures supporting martial arts that have been discussed thus far, there is little documentation of the cultural beliefs, customs, and values of the early Filipino peoples.[11] In particular, genuine historical documents from the pre-Hispanic period have been lacking and little reference to the islands has been derived from other non-European literature.[12] Indeed, in their zeal to propagate the Catholic religion, early Spanish missionaries destroyed many manuscripts on the grounds that they were the work of the Devil.[13] The absence of this cultural-historical base makes specific documentation of the evolution of the various fighting systems difficult if not virtually impossible. The general lack of specific terminology to describe select physical movements or exercises within the arts (e.g., a particular type of kick), together with teaching principles being passed on secretly within family lineages,[14] further compounds this problem. Hence, one must rely upon oral sources for this information, a procedure also being employed to investigate other aspects of Filipino culture.[15]

The art of Kali was particularly strong in the central and southern regions of the Philippines. During the Chinese Tang dynasty (A.D. 618–907), training in warrior skills as well as academic pursuits such as religion, ethics, and philosophy were allegedly conducted at an ancient school known as *Bothoan* (Bicol).[16] Implicit within the system of education and philosophy of life was the premise that both martial and non-martial aspects of life constituted the whole of existence and could not be viewed separately without distorting their role and import in the culture.

While the religion of the ancient Filipinos (Igorots, Tinguians, Bagobos) was animistic in nature, the later, higher developed Tagalog religion of Bathalaism contained an organized priesthood.[17] Aside from the influence of the Tagalog religion, early Visayan practitioners of Kali closely followed Bangka-aya's *Septalogue,* which served as law and moral guide for the people.[18] Kali was taught on three different levels: physical, mental, and spiritual. The physical level of training was generally

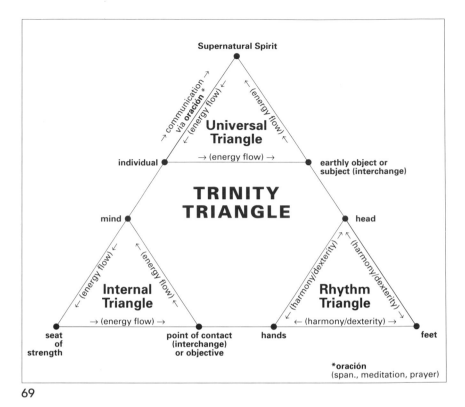

Supernatural Spirit

Universal
Triangle

communication
via oración *
→ (energy flow) ←
← (energy flow) →
→ (energy flow) ←

individual → (energy flow) → earthly object or
subject (interchange)

**TRINITY
TRIANGLE**

mind head

Internal
Triangle

← (energy flow) ←
← (energy flow) ←
→ (energy flow) →

Rhythm
Triangle

← (harmony/dexterity) →
↗ ↖ (harmony/dexterity)
(harmony/dexterity) →

seat
of
strength

point of contact
(interchange)
or objective

hands feet

*oración
(span., meditation, prayer)

69

divided into three parts that could vary from one system to another. Classifications included the following: 1. standing positions and tactics, squatting positions and tactics, lying positions and tactics; 2. long weapons, short weapons, no weapons; 3. techniques for holding weapons, projective weapons, and weaponless training. Mental training was directed to an understanding of the body, man's psychological makeup, and the role of cosmic forces. In the final, spiritual level, the Kali practitioner sought to become one with *Bathala* (Tag., God, creator, and chief deity).[19] Other terms were also used in place of Bathala, such as Creator or Supernatural Spirit.

One example of a model that incorporates these various levels and which today serves to illustrate the conceptual and structural bases of Kali, Arnis, and Eskrima is found in the Largusa-Villabrille system of Kali. Based upon principles of the triangle (Vis., *pesagi* or *tatsiha*), this system proposes the concept of a trinity triangle (Vis., *pesagi tolong*) comprised of three smaller triangles—a rhythm triangle *(pesagi pa'igon sa gawas ug kusog)*, an internal triangle *(pesagi sa labing sulod ug kusog)*, and a universal triangle *(pesagi sa tibu'ok kalibutan)*—that a practitioner could follow as a working paradigm to achieve unity and wholesomeness. A graphic illustration of this model appears as follows (Fig. 69).

Physical representation of these triangles is found in the form of exercises in this system as demonstrated here by *Tuhan* Ben T. Largusa. The rhythm triangle (Fig. 70) consists of the use of the head, hands, and feet, and employs exercises for the development of coordination and dexterity. The focus here is essentially external in nature. The rhythm triangle exercise is used to develop ambidexterity, harmony, and a good sense of rhythm. It may be performed empty-handed or with weapons. The use of weapons proves to be a more effective approach as it involves more techniques that are presented by the arm extension, more arm/stick angles, and different palm positions of both hands. The practitioner gains freedom when he has achieved the ability to apply aspects associated with all three corners of the rhythm triangle in a single unified fashion. With this freedom, one will be able to move freely and focus one's concentration on the assailant's movements. This exercise is also useful for developing external energy. The incorporation of three fighting methods of the Largusa-Villabrille Kali system—the *numerado*

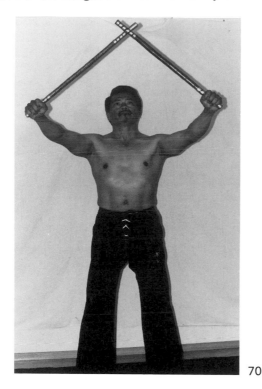

70

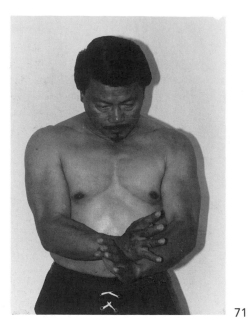

method, the *cabisedario* method, and the *sumbrada* method—enables the practitioner to attain a solid foundation of ambidexterity, harmony, and rhythm as derived from exercises that have been integrated from these three methods. The *numerado* method involves techniques practiced at arm's length with an opponent; the *cabisedario* method is practiced at double arm's length; and the *sumbrada* method encompasses counter-for-counter techniques and may incorporate both the *numerado* and *cabisedario* methods.

The internal triangle (Fig. 71) involves the use of the mind, "seat of strength" ("energy" localized in the body), and a third "point of contact" (or objective) where energy is interchangeably transmitted and retranslated between mind and body. Subsumed within this triangle are such processes as focusing, breathing, and concentration, which lead to the development of internal energy. The practitioner gains control of the flow of this energy when he has successfully integrated and applied aspects associated with the three corners of the triangle in a single unified fashion. Then, in turn, one becomes free to fully concentrate his combined internal and external energy on the point of contact. Note that the hands are open and fingers extended to allow the internal energy to continuously flow. The focus here, mentally and visually, is on the wrists, wherein, utilizing the principles of opposite directional force,

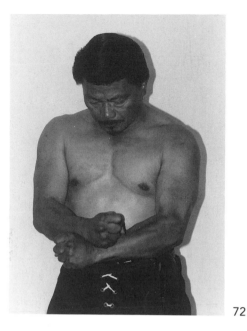

72

resistance of one wrist against another is applied. This exercise is done slowly according to a cycle that is governed by one's length of breath. It is good for developing powerful open-handed strikes and is valuable to the practitioner who is interested in breaking boards and bricks as part of his training. The arms and hands are also developed through an isometric principle of directing force against force, exerting minimal and maximal pressure at various stages. When the arms or hands are together, concentration is focused on the hands, fingers, wrists, elbows, arms, shoulder joints, or any point in the arms and hands that one wishes to develop. Both deep breathing and light normal breathing are incorporated within these exercises. When the hands are separated, concentration is focused outward toward the opponent or object through the fingers. A variation of this exercise is performed with clenched fists (Fig. 72). The purpose here is to develop powerful grabbing techniques and closed-fist striking techniques. Note that the hands are closed and fingers are locked. This allows the energy to build up to a maximal level and, having no outlet, it circulates in a whirlpool fashion within the fists. As the practitioner focuses his concentration on the wrists, the objective here is to squeeze out as much air as possible from within his fists. Both open- and closed-fist variations are performed in the same manner, and may be done with eyes either open or closed.

73

The universal triangle (Fig. 73) is essentially spiritual in form. It consists of the individual, Supernatural Spirit, and any earthly object or subject as a third point of contact. It involves communication between the individual practitioner and the Supernatural Spirit as well as an interchangeable energy flow (Vis., *dalan sa kusog*) along the third point of contact. Specific supernatural prayers *(oracion)* enable the practitioner to maintain communication with the Supernatural Spirit. Staying in tune with the Supernatural Spirit is important in order to maintain a good energy flow. As reflected in the trinity triangle, the energy flow starts from the assailant, whose energy is drawn by the Supernatural Spirit, and transmitted to the practitioner. The practitioner, in turn, retransmits this energy to the assailant. As a result, the retransmitted energy, coupled with the assailant's combined internal and external energy allows the practitioner to become twice as strong and powerful. This exercise is called *halad* and is performed in a slow manner, incorporating heavy breathing and light normal breathing with concentration directed to different parts of the body and to the Supernatural Spirit.

Principles and exercises associated with the three triangles are applied in varying degrees by the practitioner at different stages of advancement. The final goal is to bring all three triangles together until they become one triangle, the trinity triangle. It is at this point that the Kali practitioner becomes in tune with all material and spiritual aspects of the universe. The mind, in turn, becomes clear, free, devoid of thoughts or need for concentration.[20] The attainment of enlightenment (Vis., *angay*

74

imo dunong) is essentially the same as the formation of the trinity triangle. However, within Kali, the achievement of complete enlightenment
cannot be gained without studying the physical aspects or mechanics of
the art, as the practitioner would not be able to associate the physical
aspects with the theories of the trinity triangle and have those experiences emerge that are associated with its formation.[21]

To achieve this final state, a variety of meditative exercises and techniques are used within this model, including *ginhawa* (Vis., deep breathing), chanting (including the use of *mantala* [Tag., words in the way of
psalms; Skt., *mantra*] and *bulong* [Tag., whispers, prayer]), and specific
visualizations (perceiving sequences of different colors, visualizing colors
in specific parts of the body, and total bodily immersion in varied geo-
metric forms of white light). However, the specific methods or techniques used to attain the spiritual summit are not stressed, rather being
viewed simply as a means to the desired goal.[22]

An example of this tripartite connection is found in the salutation of
the Villabrille-Largusa system of Kali. Each of the movements in the
salutation are symbolic of the martial-spiritual path as follows:

> With weapons crossed in front of legs, right weapon crossed over
> the left weapon; or hands crossed in front of legs with left palm
> over the right fist (Fig. 74).

75

Preparation of *oracion:* mentally closing out the outside world and directing one's focus and concentration to the Creator or Supernatural Spirit. Presentation of oneself (Fig. 75).

Oracion: "With heaven and earth as my witness, I humbly stand before the Creator and Supernatural Spirit of light, life, and power."
Arms raised to the side and palms up; eyes open and directed upward; opening up communication with the Creator (Fig. 76).

Oracion: "In my humbleness and imperfection as an earthly subject, I pray for your forgiveness, blessing, and divine guidance."
Arms raised upward above the head to form a triangle, symbolic of the trinity triangle (Fig. 77).

Oracion: "Striving for individual oneness and universal wholesomeness as my goal, I will strive for unity within myself, mankind, and the Creator."
Triangle lowered horizontally (Fig. 78).

Oracion: "With concentration focused on the 'third eye'; with the five senses, I will strive for knowledge and wisdom through the internal triangle, the rhythm triangle, and the universal triangle."
Arms brought toward the body and crossing with the right hand inside and closer to the heart, eyes closing at the same time (Fig. 79). This signifies closing of the eyes to the outside world, and the

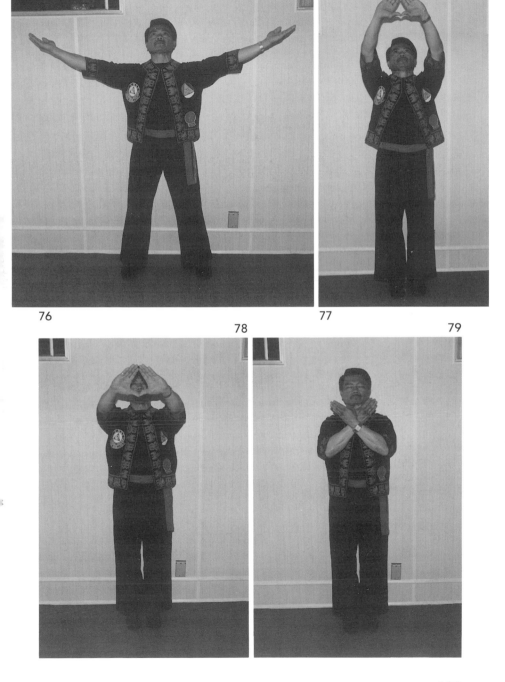

76

77

78

79

80   81

oracion is recited at this time. Special blessings are requested for
loved ones and the spirits of deceased family members. A moment
of silence is observed for the individual practitioner's special
request(s) and intention(s).

Oracion: "O, Heavenly Spirit, forgive me for all my faults and weaknesses; and, in your mercy and kindness, bless me with the spirit that will give me the guidance, strength, and power for a strong mind and body so I may develop to be a good disciple of Kali; to uphold its principles, philosophies, and its cultures."

Thanking the Creator: symbolized with the eyes open and arms extended forward with the trinity triangle (Fig. 80).

Thanking the Creator: symbolized by raising the trinity triangle upward and above the head with eyes focused on it (Fig. 81).

Oracion: "Thanking the Creator for his divine guidance as I strive for individual oneness and universal wholesomeness."

Arms lowered to the sides with palms up, eyes directed upwards to the Creator (Fig. 82).

Oracion: "In my humbleness and imperfection as an earthly subject, I thank you for your forgiveness, blessing, and divine guidance."

Lowering arms downward to the sides, return to humbleness and the outside world as an earthly subject (Fig. 83).

82

83   84   85

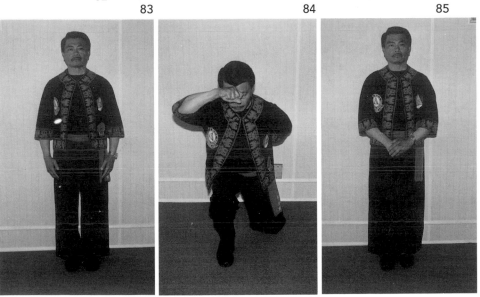

Oracion: "I stand in symbolism, for I serve only the Creator, my tribe, and my family; and I owe no allegiance to any foreign king."
With right fist at the "third eye" or weapon at forehead, signifying respect and knowledge; and the left hand to the back signifying peace and humility (Fig. 84).

Oracion: "With my mind and heart, I cherish the knowledge my instructor has given me for it is my life in combat. I bow not in submission, but in peace and respect to you."
Completion of *oracion* and salutation (Fig. 85).

A sensation of oneness with the Creator and all earthly objects and subjects is symbolized here, represented by arms crossing at front with right weapon over the left weapon or the left palm over the right fist.

Today, some fighting systems make distinctions between the internal and external aspects of the arts while others do not. Again, clearly the form and degree to which the religious goals may be stressed will vary greatly from one practitioner to another. In the case of the Filipino arts with their highly individualized systems of combat, the impact of the instructor probably carries greater weight than the principles outlined within a particular martial system. However, while the metaphysical and spiritual components exist, few practitioners are either aware of or stress this dimension in their teachings.

---

[1] Krieger, 1942
[2] Inosanto, 1980b
[3] Rausa-Gomez, 1967
[4] Cañete and Cañete, 1976; Inosanto, 1980b
[5] Inosanto, 1980b; Wiley, 1994b
[6] Hosillos, 1969; Presas, 1974; Wiley, 1994a, in press
[7] Wiley, 1994b
[8] Draeger and Smith, 1969; Inosanto, 1980b; Wiley, 1994b
[9] Inosanto, 1980b
[10] Wiley, in press
[11] Hosillos, 1969
[12] Scott, 1984
[13] Agoncillo and Alfonso, 1967
[14] Inosanto, 1980b
[15] Foronda, 1981
[16] Inosanto, 1980b; Wiley, 1994b
[17] Felipe, 1926
[18] see Nabor, 1956
[19] see Maliszewski, 1992c
[20] Ibid.
[21] Ibid.
[22] Ibid.

THAILAND

MOST WRITINGS to date suggest that the Thai race originally emigrated from central China. Earlier combative encounters were primarily with the Chinese and Mongols (thirteenth century A.D.), though later encounters with the Burmese people continued over many years. It is regrettable that with the Burmese invasion of Thailand's ancient capital of Ayutthaya in 1767, many religious relics and records concerning the origins and practices of martial activities (boxing, sword and club fighting, dancing, etc.) were destroyed. However, in many dance forms today, one can observe the use of swords, lances, *kris,* sticks, and shields.[1] Two primary combat systems found today in Thailand are Krabi-Krabong, a weapon system of sword and staff fighting, and Muay Thai (Thai Boxing). The latter tradition has the best known religious connections and, hence, will be the system discussed here.

Much of the information available today concerning earlier aspects of Muay Thai is often pieced together from contradictory information derived from writings of early European writers as well as Burmese, Cambodian, and Chinese sources. Disputes of national importance appeared to have been settled by deeds involving unarmed combat in the form of boxing, dating (traceably) back to the early 1400s. In the early part of the seventeenth century, Muay Thai comprised a part of military training. The popularity of Muay Thai reached its zenith during the reign of Pra Chao Sua, the "Tiger King" (1703–9), when it became a favorite pastime of the people. At this time, many of the teachers were Buddhist monks who viewed training in the sport as an aspect of the standard educational curriculum.[2]

One of the earliest recorded events highlighting the effects of Thai boxing took place in Burma in 1774. In Rangoon, a famous Thai boxer, Nai Knanom Tom, participated in an exhibition where he reportedly defeated nine Burmese boxers, leaving an imprint on Burmese history known even today. Several years later, in 1778, two French boxers traveled to Bangkok to challenge Thai fighters and were summarily defeated by Muen Phlaan, a teacher of the art of Thai boxing. This event further served to spread knowledge of this martial art outside its country of origin.[3]

In early times, Thai boxing made use of the hands, feet, knees, elbows, and even the head in combative encounters. In 1921, a boxing stadium was created to formally organize weekly competitions. At this time, hands were wrapped in horsehide, hemp, and later cotton threads woven loosely into a pattern that were knotted at the fingertips in a whorl. The wrapped hand was then dipped into glue and sprinkled with ground glass or grit to develop a hard, abrasive surface. This procedure served as a method of self-protection as well as a way to inflict damage on an opponent. Groin cups consisted of tree bark or sea shells held in place by a piece of cloth. Training methods could include kicking banana trees, kneeing and elbowing while swimming, and long-distance running. Fights would consist of eleven rounds lasting three minutes each. A single referee judged the outcome of the competition. Modern modifications were introduced in the 1930s and 1940s when rules and regulations from international boxing were introduced as were modern boxing gloves and other protective equipment. Some have argued that this development led to the death of traditional Muay Thai and the emergence of a new sport form that is often over-commercialized today.

At the present time, fights take place in a square ring measuring between twenty and twenty-four feet across. Each of five rounds last three minutes apiece with a two-minute time period between each round. Outcome of the fight is determined by a referee judge and two score judges sitting outside the ring. The use of musical instruments (Javanese clarinet, cymbals, and drums) also accompanies the boxing matches.[4]

Muay Thai is a hard, external art that makes use of punches, elbow strikes, kicks delivered by the knees or feet, holds, and throws. An example of a classic Muay Thai fighting technique is demonstrated here by *Aa-chan* Surachai Sirisute. His opponent delivers a punch that Sirisute blocks with his left forearm (Fig. 86) while simultaneously striking the opponent in the face with his left elbow *(ti-sok)* (Fig. 87). The technique is continued by raising the right arm (Fig. 88) and delivering a second elbow strike to the opponent's face (Fig. 89).

The connection between Buddhism and Muay Thai can be seen today in many of its traditional customs and rites. Before an individual is allowed to join a boxing camp, an entrance ritual known as the *wai-khru* must be performed in which the student's thoughts are directed toward his teacher (Figs. 90–94). It is held before a shrine *(san-phra-*

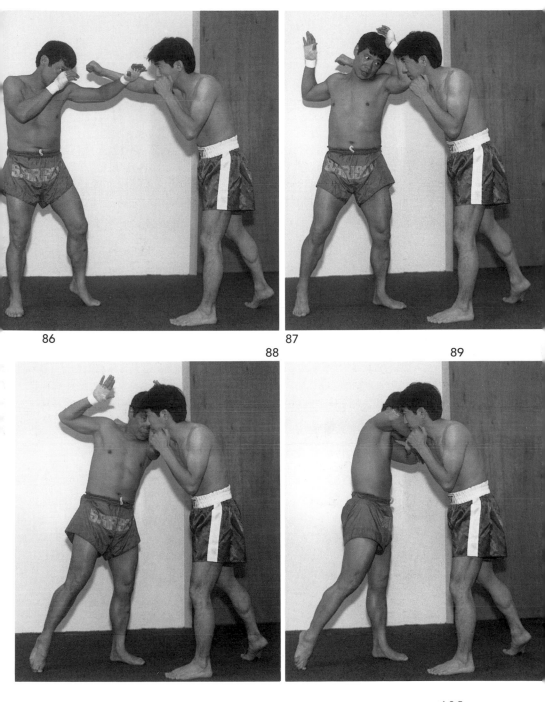

86

87

88

89

phum)—allegedly housing the guardian spirit of a particular compound—flanked on either side by Muay Thai equipment, where a student makes an offering of flowers, a piece of white cloth, joss sticks, candles, coins, or small presents before reciting a pledge of loyalty. This is followed by a period of meditation *(phaw-wa-na)*, Buddhist rituals, chants *(suad)*, and talks by the teacher and master of ceremonies. Before an actual fight, the fighter performs the *wai khru* to music, kneeling in the ring facing the direction of his camp, home, or birthplace. He then covers his eyes with his gloves and recites a short prayer while bowing low three times so that his gloves touch the canvas. This is followed by the boxing dance known as *ram-muay*. The *ram-muay* can be performed in a variety of ways and serves as a warm-up exercise and to keep evil spirits *(phi)* away. Its performance may be accompanied by silent prayers *(wai phra)* and recitation of magic formulae (Thai, *mon;* Pali, *mantra)* to assist in fighting performance and self-protection.[5]

At this time, the boxer also wears a headband known as *mong-kon* that belongs to the fighter's teacher *(khru-muay)* and is considered to be sacred. The *mong-kon* consists of a narrow strip of cloth which contains magical letters and symbols and is tightly rolled to resemble a finger-thick cord that is then tied with thread. A second strip of cloth blessed by a master is then wrapped around the first strip and twisted into a coil, the ends of which form a tail and face the back of the boxer's head. The *mong-kon* serves as a protective charm believed to provide the fighter with protection against various dangers. The *mong-kon* is removed by the trainer just prior to the first round of the fight. During an actual fight, a boxer may wear a string or piece of cloth around one or both biceps *(praciat,* armbands) that contain protective charms *(khruang-rang)*, a picture of a saint or the Buddha, or an herb said to have magic properties that serve to impart power and strength and provide protection during a fight. In the past, Thai warriors wore the *praciat* around their arms or their heads to ward off dangers encountered on the battlefield. Old drawings also depicted these warriors wearing shirts with magical letters and symbols, sashes with magical numbers and designs, and possessing tattoos on their bodies.[6]

As to the relationship between Thai Buddhism and Thai Boxing today, in rural settings some monks will teach such skills for purposes of discipline and self-defense in monasteries *(wat)* to young boys who live with them (known as *luk-sit)*. While enlightenment *(kham-ru-chaeng)* is a goal of the monk, Muay Thai is not viewed as a vehicle by which this goal can be attained. To this end, the practice of formal meditation such

90

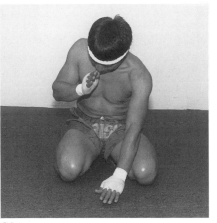
91

92

93

94

as *samathi* (Thai; *samadhi,* Pali; one-point concentration) is reserved for the monk. However, lay persons as well as Thai boxers can become monks. To the extent that modern innovations have been introduced, the importance of religious associations appears to have been minimized. However, future systematic research into martial-meditative connections is still warranted.

---

[1] Stockmann, 1979
[2] Draeger and Smith, 1969; Stockmann, 1979
[3] Kraitus and Kraitus, 1988
[4] Kraitus and Kraitus, 1988; Stockmann, 1979
[5] Stockmann, 1979
[6] Kraitus and Kraitus, 1988; Miller, 1990; Stockmann, 1979

BRAZIL

WHILE THE martial arts of various Asian countries have emigrated to South America, indigenous fighting systems can be found in select regions throughout the country. Perhaps the most widely known art from this part of the world is Capoeira, the primary African-Brazilian martial art of northeastern Brazil.

As with many martial arts, there is no definitive information concerning the origins of Capoeira. One theory suggests that African slaves sent to Brazil developed the art during the seventeenth century to aid in rebellions and escapes. Since martial training was forbidden by masters, slaves disguised the combative movements as a dance. Over the years, Capoeira was associated with lower social class stereotypes known as *malandragem* (Port.; e.g., gamblers, beggars, individuals with no visible means of support). Running battles between police officers and practitioners of Capoeira were not uncommon during the nineteenth century to the point that in 1890 a law was passed specifically prohibiting the practice of the art. Over time, the attitude held toward Capoeira shifted, beginning with the founding of the first formal academy for teaching Capoeira as a martial art. The academy *(academia)* known as Cultura Fisica de Capoeira Regional was founded in 1927 by *Mestre* Bimba (Manoel dos Reis Machado) and was the catalyst that inspired other *mestres* (senior teachers) to bring the art from the streets into the studios. In 1937, Bimba's academy was officially licensed by the government, which, in turn, led to the institutionalization of Capoeira as a sport.[1] It was not until 1972, however, that Capoeira was proclaimed a Brazilian national sport.[2]

Capoeira has a dancelike, acrobatic movement style that is combined with the presence of music and song. The art takes on the form of a game being played as a performance that can attract many kinds of spectators, both locals and tourists alike.[3] On a physical level, Capoeira makes use of attacks *(ataque)*, counterattacks *(contragolpe)*, defenses *(defesa)*, and escapes *(esquiva)* involving foot sweeps *(resteira)*, tripping, or off-balancing maneuvers *(desequilibrante)*, takedowns *(arrastao)*, front

kicks *(bencao)*, standing spinning kicks *(meia lua de compasso)*, jumping spinning kicks *(parafuso)*, cartwheels *(au)*, headspins *(piao)*, and head-butts *(cabecada)*. *Mestre* Marcelo Pereira (Fig. 95) is pictured here demonstrating the *parafuso* (propeller), a jumping spinning kick unique to Capoeira. A distinctive feature of Capoeira is the noticeable absence of hand strikes and reliance on kicks as well as a unique movement base. It has been speculated that this is due to slaves' hands being chained together or the necessity of disguising the martial aspects to make it appear more as a dance.

In contrast to many martial arts that employ a static set of stances or bases from which fighting techniques are executed, Capoeira has a moving base known as the *ginga* from which a practitioner's movements emanate (Fig. 96). All moves flow from the *ginga*, the qualities of which inform all a player's moves. The *ginga* can be divided into three parts—the *passada* (footwork), the *balanco* (bobbing forwards and backwards), and the *jogo de corps*, which involves twisting the torso from side to side and positioning and moving the hands and arms so as to distract the opponent while protecting oneself. In Capoeira, movements can function as either attacks, defenses, or both at the same time.

96

97

The space or area where Capoeira is played is always defined in terms of a circular ring of varying dimensions known as the *roda* (wheel or ring) (Fig. 97). In street locales, the ring can be formed by observers or players watching the action. In tournaments, a ring of a fixed diameter of 2.5 meters is drawn on the ground. As Capoeira is always performed to music, some players will play musical instruments and sing around the perimeter of the ring while others will "play" the physical part of the sport inside the ring. In most cases, those playing a musical instrument on the outside of the *roda* will also enter into the ring from time to time.[4]

Tactical timing in this art stresses the importance of control in playing the game of Capoeira *(jogo)*. A player attempts to control an adversary and does not allow himself to be controlled. One way of doing this is by denying an opponent space to move. Forcing a player out of the ring or surrounding him within the ring is an assertion of control over the play space. In an effort not to be controlled, the *jogador* (player of the game) performs movements known as *fechar o corpo* (to close the body) which keeps the opponent from entering his physical (and spiritual) space.[5]

There are two major Capoeira styles and an emerging style found in the contemporary practice of this Afro-Brazilian art: Angola, Regional, and Atual. The traditional style of Capoeira Angola (Kimbundu [African], integrated into Brazilian Port.) places an emphasis upon freedom of expression and individuality and is learned through observation and imitation of other practitioners. *Mestre* Vincente Ferreira Pastinha is perhaps best known for his dedication to preserving the old, traditional Angola style in the midst of the growing popularity of *Mestre* Bimba's Regional style. Capoeira Regional was developed and structured for the purpose of perpetuating the art to the diverse groups of students who enrolled in the Capoeira *academias*. Regional practices include sequences of required movements *(sequencia)*, standardized methods of learning the movements, and responding to movements primarily in self-defense situations. The contemporary emerging style of Capoeira is known as Atual (Port., modern, current, up to date). Capoeira Atual is a progressive style initiated by *Mestre* No (Norival Moreira de Oliveira) and is used to refer to those styles that combine Regional contributions with the more traditional Angola components. The Atual style emerged as a response by *capoeiristas* to unify their art into "one Capoeira."[6]

Depicted here are two stylistic techniques found within the repertoire of Capoeira Angola and Capoeira Regional respectively. Unique to Capoeira Angola is the movement known as *gueda de rins* (fall on the kidneys), a kind of headstand using the side of the head with one elbow bent onto the kidney area for support (Fig. 98). This movement may be found in the "dancelike" *jogo* and may be used as a kind of greeting or training movement, although a kick may certainly be executed from this position. As a defense against the front heel kick *(bencao)*, the practitioner of Capoeira Regional executes the *rasteira* (sweeping technique), which is used to take the opponent's feet out from underneath him (Fig. 99). The Regional style makes use of a variety of high jumping and spinning kicking techniques as well as acrobatic flips and cartwheels.

Capoeira Angola bears a historical though indirect relationship to Candomble, the African-Brazilian religion of Bahia (Brazil). Even prior to the abolition of slavery in 1888, Capoeira was alleged to have been

98

99

"played" before and after *candomble* ceremonies.[7] *Capoeiristas* (Brazilian Port., players of Capoeira) have been linked to *orixas,* spirits of the (African) Yoruba tradition who enter the heads of initiates and cause them to sing and dance while entranced.[8] To gain acceptance by slave owners, slaves syncretized their African traditional beliefs with Catholicism. Each *orixas* has an equivalent Catholic saint as an alter ego. Through the "spiritual works" practiced by religious leaders called *pais de santo* (Brazilian Port., "father of the saints") or *maes de santo* (Brazilian Port., "mothers of the saints"), the bodies of *capoeiristas* would reportedly become impenetrable to knives and bullets.

Prior to entering the *roda,* the *jogadores* touch the ground and begin to concentrate and then enter a preliminary trance wherein begins the

100

body movements that define the "game of Capoeira."[9] It is the rhythm of the various musical instruments played that effect the trancelike state. The primary instruments of Capoeira are the *berimbau* (musical bow), *caxixi* (woven rattle played with the *berimbau*), *reco-reco* (ribbed bamboo scraper), and *agogo* (two-tone clapperless bell or gong).[10]

At the onset of a *jogo* or "game of Capoeira," the most senior *mestre* will sing an introductory solo or litany known as the *ladainha*, which is immediately followed by the *chula* (special introductory song). Today, in a circle of Capoeira, when two *capoeiristas* bend down in front of the *berimbau* (the central percussion instrument used in Capoeira) to "play" Capoeira, they make a reverent gesture to the *berimbau*, bless themselves (make the sign of the cross), evoke the ballads that describe the feats of the ancient *capoeiras* (an older term for *capoeiristas*), and pray to God and the master who taught them. (Some at this point may pray privately to the *orixas* although this is not a formal part of the ritual practice.)

Depicted here is the three-step ritual sequence which begins the *jogo* or "game of Capoeira": 1. Two *capoeiristas* (*Mestre* Gladson on right) bend down assuming the *cocorinha* (squatting) posture (Fig. 100). *Mestre* Gladson describes the practice as follows: "At this moment I am ab-

101   102

sorbed in the sound of the instruments singing a prayer or litany telling
of the past masters and their feats." At this moment, the *berimbau* is
played using the Angola beat, a slow beat for concentration that leads to
berravento (a pre-possession trance state). 2. An improvised song is begun here (Fig. 101). "I am quite involved in the rhythm of the instruments and feeling more and more in the core of my being," the words
spoken in relation to the sung 'prayer,' which are as follows:

Besouro Preto Dourado

Besouro Preto Dourado   This is the name of a great *capoeirista*
                                           who is now deceased. Literally, it
                                           means "black beetle" who was post-
                                           humously awarded the golden cord (a
                                           fictitious status as a legendary hero).

Who taught you to play?

It was *Mestre Siri de Mangue Besouro*

Manganga.   A different master (literal meaning,
                                           "swamp crab") another name for *Be-
                                           souro Preto Dourado* (literal meaning,
                                           great medicine man).

PART TWO: A DESCRIPTIVE & VISUAL SURVEY: BRAZIL   **119**

Come here *Besouro Preto.*
I am going to ask you a favor.
Come here *Besouro Preto.*
I am going to ask you a favor.
Knock down this black man,
so he will no longer be so bold.

(Bold in the sense of impudent.)

The response of the other *capoeirista* is:
Dende, oh, *Dende, Dende* with a yellow ring.

Literally, *dende* refers to palm oil or fruit of the palm; here it connotes a nickname for *capoeirista.*

I am going to show you that I am a man, not a woman.

Yellow ring indicates that *dende* is also a *capoeirista.* The palm oil leaves a yellow ring in a pot when cooking. Here yellow ring is associated with cooking, a woman's role. This *capoeirista* has a name associated with women and hence has to prove that he is a man.

3. The beginning of the game proper (Fig. 102). In this phase, the "beat of the *berimbau*" changes to the *Sao Bento Grande* (literally, Great Saint of Bento), which is more rapid, requiring very great motor coordination in the execution of the Capoeira movements.

It should be pointed out with the passage of time that Capoeira has continued to become more separate from *candomble* and its practices. It remains unclear whether or not this trend that de-emphasizes religious-cultural practices will continue to persist. As noted with other martial arts, the religious associations that are or have been a part of Capoeira are in need of systematic investigation. Here, given the limited written documentation, studies need to be conducted before these practices are completely lost with the passage of time.

---

[1] Almeida, 1982
[2] Lewis, 1986, 1992
[3] Lewis, 1992
[4] Ibid.
[5] Ibid.
[6] see Lewis, 1986
[7] Rego, 1968
[8] Evleshin, 1986; Lewis, 1986
[9] Maliszewski, 1992c
[10] Lewis, 1992

UNITED STATES

MANY OF the classical and contemporary martial arts described previously have been exported to the United States and have taken root there. Depending upon the attitude and orientation of the teacher of a particular art, some disciplines have remained relatively unchanged from the form originally developed by their creators. Practitioners of other systems, on the other hand, have attempted to adapt the essence of their particular style to the values held by contemporary American society, though maintaining the original name for their art. Still other stylists have significantly modified the style, techniques, principles, and orientation of their martial foundations, indicating this reformulation by applying a new name to their art. Of these many significantly modified styles, however, one approach stands out in its reference to metaphysical principles derived from Asian philosophies, namely, the art of Jeet Kune Do (or Jit Kuen Do), which was developed by the late Bruce Lee.

Born in San Francisco in 1940, Bruce Lee received much of his early training in Hong Kong. His strongest base in the martial arts consisted of his training in Wing Chun (Chin./C.; Chin./M. Yong Chun), a close-range, in-fighting Chinese *gong-fu* style.[1] A young Bruce Lee is depicted here training on the *mujen chuang* (wooden dummy), a training tool characteristic of this system (Fig. 103, p. 122).

Upon his return to the United States in 1958, he began modifying this base by borrowing techniques and principles from a wide range of different systems and traditions, including, yet not limited to, Judo, Western boxing, wrestling, Boxe Française Savate, European fencing, Karate, as well as several other *gong-fu* styles, including Praying Mantis (Chin./M., Tang Lang), Eagle Claw (Chin./M., Ying Zhao), Taijiquan, and Choy Li Fut (Chin./C.; Chin./M., Cai Li Fo).[2] Several evolutionary stages in his modified Wing Chun style—illustrated by his teachings in various geographical settings (Seattle, Oakland, and later Los Angeles)—led to his development of Jit Kuen Do (Chin./C., *jit*, to stop, to intercept; *kuen*, fist or style; *do*, Jpn./Kor. way: Way of the Intercepting Fist; customary spelling, Jeet Kune Do).[3]

103

More than an amalgam or modification of various martial arts and related combat systems, Jeet Kune Do consisted of a collection of mental and physical concepts, observations of combat maneuvers and strategies, as well as the practical application of philosophical principles derived from Zen, Confucian, and Daoist writings. Stressing practical combat as the most effective test of a technique, Lee discarded those aspects of fighting traditions that he deemed superfluous or impractical. Rather than stress a specific set of techniques or particular style, however, Lee emphasized the absence of stereotyped techniques. Jeet Kune Do was an approach best described as alive, fluid, and continually adapting.[4] The practice of this art stressed the importance of the practitioner over the art form: the goal was to select those techniques, principles, and philosophical premises that best fit the individual practitioner's physical, mental, and spiritual makeup.[5] Hence, the expression of Jeet Kune Do was an individual one, best tailored to the individual's knowledge of martial techniques, setting, and psychophysical constitution. Lee's approach, clearly non-classical in its orientation, created a controversy among the more contemporary classical stylists.[6] Writings by his earliest students clearly illustrate the radical changes he brought to the classical discipline of Wing Chun,[7] and later works by other pupils illustrate the constant evolution of his art.[8] Furthermore, his fighting skills were reported to be extraordinary.[9]

To illustrate a conceptual application of this art, Bruce Lee's protégé, Dan Inosanto, is depicted here with the author demonstrating a Jeet Kune Do fighting sequence of three types of techniques (opening, follow-up, and finishing techniques) spontaneously blending the different component parts traditionally associated with different martial arts. First, the opponent (right) punches to *Guro* Inosanto's head, while Inosanto cross-parries and hits the opponent's inner forearm (Fig. 104). The opponent's arm is trapped with the left hand (Fig. 105) and Inosanto backfists to his face with his right hand (Fig. 106). The opponent blocks with his rear hand (Fig. 107). Inosanto grabs this hand with his left

104

105

106

107

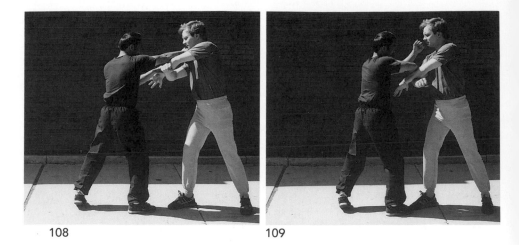

108   109

hand and delivers a right backfist to the opponent's face (Fig. 108). Inosanto's right arm then presses down on both of the opponent's arms, trapping them so that a face punch can be delivered with Inosanto's left hand without obstruction (Fig. 109). The following movements are generally associated with specific arts: (Figs. 104, 105—Kali; Figs. 106, 107—Jeet Kune Do; Figs. 108, 109—Wing Chun).

The philosophical aspects of Lee's unorthodox approach were largely derived from Daoist and Zen precepts as well as the more contemporary influences of Krishnamurti.[10] As with the martial aspects of his teachings, strong emphasis was placed upon the importance of practical application of these principles, both psychologically and physically. Similar to the physical component, Lee's interpretations and understanding of such terms as enlightenment, voidness, nothingness, consciousness of self, and other related concepts bore his own unique imprint. His early use of meditation appeared to be primarily geared to enhancing his skills and performance in the physical domain.

Despite this early utilitarian stance, the evolution of Lee's modified Wing Chun to Jeet Kune Do also began to permeate his practice of meditation. Early exercises involved a traditional Chinese *gong-fu* approach—practicing diaphragmatic breathing in horse stance *(ma bu)* position to cultivate *qi* below the navel in the *dantien.*[11] Lee viewed this region as a power source and the center of gravity of the body. Concentration upon this area of the body was preceded by freeing the mind of all thoughts, "mirroring" the mind (i.e., allowing perceptions, sensations, thoughts, and emotions to come and go as a mirror reflects images back to the perceiver). Believing in the limitations of this set physical-meditative approach to direct combative applications, yet using it as a preliminary foundation, Lee later began to advocate moving this power base and center of gravity to other parts of the body (e.g., chest area) depending upon the situation in which the individual found himself and the repertoire of fighting techniques needed to overcome an opponent. Opposing set response patterns, the opponent's techniques determined what techniques Lee would then follow through with (i.e., "your technique is my technique").[12] Later Lee illustrated this flexibility on a physical level by sparring with opponents and defeating them in pre-selected fighting style approaches (sometimes the opponent's own style) as well as switching spontaneously through various styles or techniques of particular martial arts throughout a sparring session. At this point in his development, Lee viewed the role of the mind as primary, *qi* as being relegated to a secondary position of medium through which adrenaline might be tapped. Unfortunately, later students did not attend closely to the specific meditative techniques or strategies Lee employed at more advanced stages of his practice.[13] However, sitting meditation did comprise one of these practices (Fig. 110).

Some accounts given by students and associates suggest that a char-

110

acterological authentication or transformation did not constitute an effect of Lee's training.[14] Later in his career, meditation constituted a regular part of his daily martial arts practice schedule. However, the emphasis upon continuous improvement or further development in his philosophy remained as illustrated by two of his best known adages: 1. "Using no Way as Way, having no limitation as limitation," and 2. "the pursuit of becoming from moment to moment" and constantly searching and questioning whether one is truthful to oneself and one's own pursuit.[15] Clearly, cultural influences were in play here: the perspective of continuous development reflects the attitude held by most martial arts practitioners in present-day China and Hong Kong, and Lee's eclectic, individual-centered approach further depicts salient features of the American cultural environment.

Given the devotion and intensity Lee brought to his art, it would be expected that, had he not died prematurely, the nature of his Jeet Kune Do would have evolved even more dramatically than it had in its earlier stages—probably toward greater simplicity and, possibly, spirituality. Since Jeet Kune Do varied from one individual to another (according to Lee's philosophy), the serious consideration given to the meditative-religious elements would vary greatly from one practitioner to another. The art most certainly would not have been closed to this dimension.[16] To date, however, contemporary writings of his students and followers have not stressed this area,[17] although exceptions to this trend can be found.[18] Clearly, the final story has not yet been told about this enigmatic art as well as Lee's contributions to the martial arts in general.

---

[1] see Cheung, 1983, 1985; Leung, 1978; Wong, 1976
[2] Glover, 1976; Vunak, 1985
[3] Cheung and Wong, 1990; Inosanto, 1976; Lee and Campbell, in press
[4] see Inosanto, 1986b; Vunak, 1985
[5] Inosanto, 1976; B. Lee, 1975
[6] see Inosanto, 1976; Lee, 1971/1986; Uyehara, 1988
[7] DeMile, 1977; Glover, 1976
[8] Inosanto, 1976, 1980a, 1982
[9] Borine, in preparation; Clouse, 1988; Thomas, 1994
[10] see B. Lee, 1975
[11] for a perspective on this approach, see Wong, 1978, pp. 47–48

[12] see Maliszewski, 1992c
[13] Ibid.
[14] see Clouse, 1987; L. Lee, 1975, p. 199; Maslak, 1979
[15] Lau, 1981
[16] see B. Lee, 1975, p. 200; Lee and Bleeker, 1989, pp. 36–41
[17] see Beasley, 1989, 1992; Glover, 1981; Hartsell, 1984; Hartsell and Tackett, 1987; Inosanto, 1980a, 1982; Kent and Tackett, 1986, 1988; Segal, 1984
[18] see Silliphant, 1970; Hyams, 1979

PART THREE

A Re-Assessment of Martial Arts
and
Spiritual Traditions

By its very nature, the internal is cooperative. It breaks down when it becomes overly competitive. Springing from Daoism and Buddhism, it stresses being and becoming rather than thinking and doing. Learning is aided if one remembers that there is no opponent—only ourselves.

However, the internal is not a gift: it must be worked for, and discipline is necessary (an old text runs, "An inch of meditation, an inch of Buddha"). But even this is largely cooperative. Too often what passes for discipline becomes sadistic (on the part of the teacher) or masochistic (on the part of the student). Many martial arts taught today, in Asia as well as the West, tend toward the sociopathic on this score. What is wanted is a good balance.

—Robert W. Smith

I told him of the chow-mein cooks now teaching Kung-Fu and the young and old Indians posing as gurus abroad in America. "That is always the way," he mused sadly. "Those who know not, teach, and those who know are unknown."

—John F. Gilbey

(Overleaf). *Sifu* T.T. Liang demonstrates the *Shang Pu Qi Xing* (Step Forward to the Seven Stars) posture from Yang Taijiquan.

INFORMATION PRESENTED in the preceding section reveals that, for many martial arts, the connection between the meditative and martial traditions is indisputable. However, contemporary relationships between these two fields, particularly in the United States, are less than complementary. Generally acknowledged masters of the martial arts may not have any understanding of or experience within a formal meditative discipline, particularly those features associated with the culmination of a meditative path. Indeed, as noted earlier, mastery within a particular martial art may always be viewed as incomplete, where one's practice never reaches an optimal point of development. The implication here is that there is always a higher level to which one can aspire.[1] Many experienced practitioners exhibit behavioral features, personality traits, and a general level of psychological maturity indistinguishable from a neophyte in the art. In this vein, while an authentic martial arts master can distinguish the physical competence of a movement or set of movements by a highly advanced technician from that of an acknowledged master (in terms of mind-body coordination and performance),[2] it is quite rare to find a corresponding qualitative assessment made of the practitioner's consciousness, psychological development, and degree of advancement along a spiritual path. The evaluation of the noncorporeal, intangible ego remains elusive, and attention is devoted instead (by those more mystically minded) to more comforting concepts of "energy" or (by the realists) to the perfection of select psychophysical techniques. In such martial arts, the only parallel that exists to certain meditative traditions is the external formality of the pupil's deference to his teacher, symbolic of the latter's greater skill and experience.

Within various schools of martial arts, a very small number of practitioners value the role of formal meditation as an adjunctive method of realizing one's essential nature or attaining optimal psychological development (enlightenment). Some other groups recognize the spiritual dimension of the martial arts, but due to the need for emphasis upon the physical foundations, do not directly employ meditative exercises as part of their training. In yet other systems, a brief sitting session is included before and/or after a workout or training session as a means of increasing relaxation, heightening perception, building self-confidence and self-discipline, promoting mind-body integration, or imparting an "Eastern" flavor to the art. Finally, still other practitioners dismiss the need for the spiritual or meditative dimension altogether.

It is appropriate to ask what the purpose is of pursuing the practice of martial arts and further, of being involved in the meditative disciplines today. Aside from the reasons given in the introduction, many practitioners describe an emotional "pull" or intrinsically rewarding connection to their martial art, which, upon analysis, stems from a complex interplay of physical, psychological, and social factors. Indeed, many practitioners pursue further study with an enthusiasm, tenacity, and conviction that transcend concerns with combative skill.

Donohue has suggested that the allure of martial arts stems from the fact that they constitute ritual performances that symbolically deal with the fundamental questions of human existence: mortality and the quest for control, mystery, the hunt for power, and the search for identity.[3] Our sense of mortality is heightened by increased fears of street violence and dissatisfaction with society. The symbolic recreation of danger through practice of the martial arts can provide us with the illusion of control over such events. The mysterious component of Asian martial arts is often associated with the development of paranormal skills nestled in a matrix of "occult knowledge" that transcends everyday life experiences. The ongoing practice and rehearsal of techniques coupled with the review of underlying philosophical precepts serves to foster a sense of individual and personal accomplishment. Participation in practices with a large group of people sharing common beliefs provides an individual with a greater sense of identity as well as a sense of place and purpose in life. One seeks to integrate and "ground" oneself on each of these different levels: physical, psychological, social, and metaphysical.

A natural progression and extension of practice is to continue to reinforce and intensify these positive experiences. Meditative-spiritual practices serve their function by offering further characterological changes and transcendent possibilities, which likely account for their elevated position at the most advanced stages of martial practice. A member of a society searching for meaning and purpose can achieve this goal through the re-enactment of these highly personal performances. The practitioner is simultaneously able to strengthen his connection with everyday reality and to acquire methods of transcending its limitations.

Nonetheless, a general problem that exists among many consummate practitioners of the martial arts is the degree to which they are absorbed in the physical dimensions of the arts to the exclusion of the spiritual, religious, and/or meditative components (not to mention also cultural and philosophical influences). The martial arts literature is replete with stories of practitioners who are attracted to the arts by personal feelings of physical impotence and by an inability to successfully defend themselves physically against an aggressor. This may emerge from a single traumatic physical altercation they have had or from being raised in an environment in which successful acquisition of one's needs for security and mastery in the world was achieved through physical force and strength. To overcome fears, anxieties, and a sense of inadequacy associated with being physically and psychologically powerless, they choose to study a martial art. While several years' practice may provide the necessary skill needed to avert the threat of physical violence, the psychological development and maturation that often accompany exposure to religious teachings and meditative practices do not follow. Hence, what may emerge are proficient practitioners whose psychological growth remains fixed at an earlier developmental stage. The focus of such practitioners is to amass more knowledge of techniques and their applications (within a single system or across several disciplines), awaiting the time when such a viable repertoire of fighting skill will need to be applied. The continuing pursuit and accumulation of the "physical" knowledge reinforces the need for more practice and more knowledge, since the original conflict that initially motivated the pursuit of this type of activity has never been explored and resolved through understanding, natural maturation, or therapeutic intervention. Individuals who fall into this path have little awareness of any alternative methods outside of their training for dealing with physical threats to their physical well-being. The psychological attitude such practitioners have about themselves, their relationships with other people, and their broader perspective on life go unnoticed, superseded by their fixation with physical practice. Indeed, training in the martial arts may serve as a particularly attractive compensatory strategy when it is construed as non-psychological practice, i.e., as a discipline that is essentially physical and not involving thoughtfulness and self-reflection. Many people who feel powerless and inadequate find it painful and humiliating to pay attention to such feelings, let alone to understand them and resolve such conflicts therapeutically. Physical prowess achieved through martial arts may actually become an organizing metaphor for a variety of social as well as internal psychological concerns and fears.

Unknown to a vast majority of martial arts practitioners is the extent to which many of the martial arts at various periods in time historically drew upon meditative and religious principles (derived from written sources, oral transmissions, and/or in-body transmission through movement) to authenticate or transform the practitioner's view of himself in the cultural-societal-cosmological context in which he was rooted. Exposure to these teachings tempered (sometimes radically altered) the earlier attitudes held by the practitioner, often dissolving fears and aggressive reactions to problems. A number of classical meditative systems, such as Hindu Tantrism or religious Daoism, have addressed the radical psychological transformation of the individual and also have subsumed within their repertoire of exercises and training methods many of the same basic principles used in "internal" systems of martial arts to develop high levels of mastery in martial technique. While simple redirection of attention by a highly advanced meditator within such systems could easily lead to a rapid development of "internal" martial capabilities (e.g., within Chinese systems, deployment of *qi* in an offensive martial capacity), primary attention to the development and refinement of such skills would be viewed by the serious meditator as a deviation from the primary (experiential) goal of meditation. In contrast, the typical martial arts practitioner would view this level of attainment (e.g., the cultivation and manipulation of *qi* as an end goal in and of itself) as falling within the category of "mastery" in many of the contemporary martial arts traditions.

At this time, the limited number of writings that address the use of meditation in the martial arts generally stress the practical impact it can have in such areas as reducing tension or tonic muscle activity, coping with stress, and increasing self-control and attention in physical movement. This view parallels the focus of empirical behavioral studies that often seek to measure the psychological and physiological changes that take place over time with the practice of meditation. However, an increased number of writings have pointed to the fact that these behavioral changes may have little to do with the stated goals of authentic classical and contemporary meditative disciplines and contemplative traditions, the phenomenological components and goals bearing far greater importance.[4] It is to this end that scholars involved in research on meditation can serve a most important role, namely, reacquainting martial arts practitioners and researchers with the meditative dimension of the martial arts in general, including the depth, complexity, and nature of the goals associated with these systems. The mind is acknowledged by many practitioners as being of central importance to their art.[5] However, the experiential elements associated with the classical meditative goals often remain unrecognized.

It is worthwhile to note here that the effects of martial-based movements upon the mind can range in intensity across several categories including triggering an alteration in the customary level of awareness; as a means to develop concentration, to cultivate mindfulness and insight, or to empty the mind of conscious thoughts; as a direct method of attaining enlightenment; or as the symbolic representation of a goal associated with the culmination of a meditative path.[6] The respective impact will vary as a function of the physical constitution, psychological makeup, and orientation of the practitioner, the specific technique(s) employed as well as the interaction of technique with practitioner.

Furthermore, the ways in which the experience of meditation unfolds and affects the practitioner can also vary among different meditative systems, including approaches that articulate the progressive changes in consciousness as outlined in select classical texts and contemporary literature;[7] other systems that have a different phenomenological flavor emphasizing the way of "sudden" enlightenment;[8] teachings that consist of variations on the theme of sudden versus gradual enlightenment (e.g., sudden enlightenment followed by gradual cultivation; gradual cultivation followed by sudden enlightenment; sudden cultivation and sudden enlightenment, etc.);[9] other traditions that have renounced all methods and dichotomies of sudden versus progressive enlightenment;[10] and teachings of the "great perfection" (Tibetan, *rdzog'-chen*).[11]

In reality, subsuming phenomenological experiences based on martial and meditative practices within any general classification of models of consciousness may prove to be difficult. To begin, the conscious, repetitive practice of select physical movements over time becomes encoded on an unconscious level within the mind of the practitioner. Response to a physical threat or movement with martial techniques may involve no conscious awareness on the part of the practitioner nor strict rote re-enactment of previously learned movements (i.e., subliminal or unconscious intentions and specific [yet possibly varied] movement patterns bypass the individual's introspective, conscious awareness altogether). While such exercises and responses are actually "meditative" in nature (even if overtly practiced only with an emphasis upon physical performance), the practitioner may not consciously identify them as such. Introduction of formally defined meditative or religious practices further compounds the problem of analyzing purely physical aspects: some martial arts encourage the further development of the subliminal senses, though the way in which this "intuition" is employed will vary (e.g., compare the meaning of the expression *kanken futatsu no koto* as it is understood in classical *bujutsu* and classical *budo* forms noted by Draeger).[12] Other practices, in contrast, neither cultivate increased consciousness of such processes nor associate it with orthodox combat systems (e.g., the spontaneous movement of *karaga* found in Java).[13] As one might surmise, martial-based meditative disciplines can contribute to shifts in psychological functioning that are not observed in similar, non-martial meditative disciplines. The form and degree to which such "unconscious" elements and other characterological changes occur in the practice of formal martial, meditative, or martial-meditative systems will involve an idiographic assessment of the person within the respective tradition or traditions.

Given the many complex factors involved in selecting a meditative or martial path and the sequence of psychosocial events that may unfold in practice, caution should be exercised in undertaking this personal exploration. This is particularly true with respect to assessing one's level of mastery in both martial and meditative realms. While misrepresentation of credentials and experience in the martial arts is an acknowledged phenomenon,[14] such misrepresentation also exists in meditative traditions as well, both historically[15] and on the contemporary scene.[16] Most writings on the topic of meditation and optimal psychological development[17] will provide the reader with a general flavor of non-martial meditative goals. However, with few exceptions,[18] phenomenological descriptions and self-reports by contemporary scholars knowledgeable in behavioral sciences and religious studies are often characterized by limited experience within even a single meditative discipline.[19] Ironically, the most widely published writers in this area are among the least experienced on the "path" and in fact are unable to either assess or understand the nature of advanced meditative experience. Such a factor can have a significant impact upon models or paradigms of consciousness experience proposed to embrace such phenomena, particularly with respect to advanced techniques and experiences.[20] While one is generally safer with classical text literature and testimonies of acknowledged (oftentimes, historical) personages in the field, a true assessment involves direct person-to-person contact and dialogue. In the martial arts, a flawless, effortless performance by a master within a particular system can either serve to illustrate direct experience and embodiment of this authenticated or transformative psychological dimension, or simply excellence in technical execution. Similarly, writings of an individual involved in a meditative tradition can range from an expression of one who has traversed the path of his discipline to simply one who projects the persona of an enlightened teacher.

Given this state of affairs, a number of suggestions can be made to strengthen the relationship between martial arts and meditative traditions, both experientially and scholastically. To begin, once the variability in range of experiential possibilities is recognized and the authenticity of respective teachers established, truly advanced meditation teachers in conjunction with knowledgeable behavioral scientists, historians of religion, and allied specialists could then proceed to suggest specific exercises to enhance and complement meditative-martial exercises already employed in particular martial arts. In virtually all of the different martial arts (and there are thousands of different styles, some still unrecorded), there are specific methods and movements that lend themselves to inducing unique qualitative shifts in consciousness and corresponding psychological functions (emotions, perceptions, etc.), improving concentration, cultivating mindfulness, "emptying" the contents of the mind, triggering various alternate states of consciousness, or eliciting the more dramatic psychological changes characteristic of enlightenment, e.g., the "moving meditation" of select martial arts, "hypnotic-trance" techniques of the Joduk and Setia Hati Terate styles of Balinese Pencak-Silat, the "spirit shout" (Jpn., *kiai*) of various martial arts, the acrobatic and gymnastic movements of Capoeira and the Japanese martial art of Taikudo, the regulation of breath, and the use of specific musical arrangements to name only a few.[21]

Unfortunately, in some circumstances (e.g., within certain modern *budo* systems), specific movements and techniques have been rigidly linked to particular styles, cultures, or traditions. I propose that the entire range of "mind-altering" martial-based exercises be made available to all styles of martial arts, regardless of the philosophical stances traditionally associated with them. Further, the goals of the various meditative systems (and their cultural-philosophical premises) should also be made available to the practitioner of martial arts, who, having a strong foundation in at least one martial art, can then be guided through careful selection of psychophysical techniques of other systems by masters of both (or better, be absorbed and integrated by a master of both) martial and formal (non-martial) meditative paths.

Some writers have argued that synthesizing styles and techniques leads to a dilution of movements or principles, thus rendering the art ineffective. While many contemporary practitioners recognize the importance of integrating and adopting techniques from various styles and arts,[22] many meditators steadfastly adhere to the practice of a single discipline, often not recognizing that "pure" forms of meditative schools are essentially ideals, even as noted in the more familiar systems of Buddhism and Hinduism.[23] Despite the inherent difficulty and the time factor involved in completing a specific meditative path, the completion and integration of several distinct meditative disciplines is an ideal position suggested here, a position that has been successfully achieved within the recent past.[24] Simple accumulation of techniques (meditative or martial) is not argued here. Rather, one should be able to draw upon a wide variety of teachings, techniques, and "experiential possibilities" that are not found within a "single" meditative tradition and that further make for a truly comprehensive psychological authentication or transformation.

From another viewpoint, martial arts can also be used to complement "static" meditative disciplines. According to legend, techniques associated with the martial arts were reportedly employed by Bodhidharma to offset the austerity of strict contemplative efforts as well as to provide the physical foundations in body development necessary to withstand the dramatic shift in consciousness that characterizes enlightenment. Today, the same position can be argued as well: the psychophysical exercises of the martial arts can both offset the strict meditative exercises with an alternative form of "moving meditation" (thus complementing one set of practice techniques with an additional group of preparatory exercises) as well as prepare the body physically to support and sustain the dramatic shifts in consciousness that lie ahead.[25] The physical practice can also serve as psychological "grounding" for those practitioners who might lose touch with activities of the external physical world, having become excessively preoccupied with their internal mentation.[26] Further, though hitherto unrecognized by many serious meditators, careful selection and practice of specific martial techniques and movements can accelerate the progress of the meditator towards his respective goal, regardless of the particular meditative discipline in which he may be involved. In contrast to these observations, most studies investigating the physical effects of practicing the martial arts have been concerned with issues of medical injury.

Historically, the attitude held by various classical meditative systems towards the martial arts has been mixed. The relationship of the arts to Buddhism, for example, has been inconsistent. Some schools teach that the tenets of Buddhist philosophy are antithetical to martial ideology, whereas others, as noted earlier, have incorporated martial components into their practice.[27]

Some questions have been raised as to the superior merit of the martial path to enlightenment. Many practitioners argue that the "moving meditation" of select martial arts are superior to the static and sitting forms observed in Yoga, Buddhism, or Daoism, even claiming support for such perspectives in early Daoist writings.[28] The great Zen master Hakuin (1685–1768) also felt that the way of the warrior could serve as a model for the monk:

> In my later years I have come to the conclusion that the advantage in accomplishing true meditation lies distinctly in favor of the warrior class. . . Mounted on a sturdy horse, the warrior can ride forth to face an uncountable horde of enemies as though he were riding into a place empty of people. The valiant, undaunted expression on his face reflects his practice of the peerless, true, uninterrupted meditation sitting. Meditation in this way, the warrior can accomplish in one month what it takes the monk a year to do; in three days he can open up for himself benefits that would take the monk a hundred days.[29]

In contrast, a contemporary view from the standpoint of one organized meditative system—religious Daoism—presents a different picture: composed of nearly one hundred different sects, the Bei-Ji (Pole Star) sect stands out in its use of *gong-fu* bodily exercises and military prowess involving spirits and weapons as a means to attaining "immortality." Despite the apparent divergence of this sect from others in its rituals and methods, most sects, at one time or another, have sought to attain this goal.[30] This example clearly fits with the historical review outlined earlier, namely, that the martial-meditative traditions as a whole allowed for much ingenuity and diversity as to how one might actualize oneself on this path.

From the information presented in this text, clearly the martial arts can be viewed as effective combat systems, sophisticated meditative disciplines, or as an integration of both approaches, the orientation depending upon the training and focus of the teacher and the goals of the student-practitioner. Admittedly, this survey has served solely as an introduction to a highly complex area of study, its purpose being to acquaint the reader with the meditative-religious components of several martial arts and the nature of the goals that characterized the spiritual dimensions of practice.

Note: The quoted selections from *Zen Master Hakuin* appear courtesy of Columbia Press Inc.

[1] Hyams, 1979, pp. 39–40
[2] see description by Draeger, 1973b, pp. 28–29
[3] Donohue, 1991
[4] Maliszewski, Twemlow, Brown, and Engler, 1981; Shapiro, 1982
[5] Fong, 1976; Glover, 1981
[6] see Maliszewski, 1992c
[7] Maliszewski, Twemlow, Brown, and Engler, 1981; Wilber, Engler, and Brown, 1986
[8] Blofeld, 1962; Stein, 1971; Yampolsky, 1967
[9] Park, 1980; Shih, 1971, p. 175
[10] see review by Dumoulin, 1953
[11] Manjusrimitra, 1986; Norbu, 1987a, 1987b
[12] Draeger, 1973b, pp. 28–30
[13] see Stange, 1980/1981   -
[14] see Draeger, 1974b; Stewart, 1980; Suh, 1986
[15] see Nagashima, 1978; Sasaki, 1975, pp. 1–39; Yampolsky, 1971, pp. 29–73

[16] Bharati, 1976; Vaughan, 1983; Welwood, 1983
[17] Shapiro, 1980b; Shapiro and Walsh, 1984; Tart, 1975b; Walsh and Shapiro, 1983; Walsh and Vaughan, 1980; Wilber, Engler, and Brown, 1986
[18] Maliszewski, in preparation
[19] see Tart, 1971; Walsh, 1977, 1978
[20] see Riebel, 1982
[21] see Maliszewski, 1992c
[22] see Beasley, 1983; Inosanto, 1982
[23] Smith, 1981
[24] see Satprem, 1968; Stark, 1974
[25] for a similar analogy on a strictly physical level, see Richards, 1982
[26] Kalb, 1977
[27] see Demieville, 1957, for a detailed analysis of this association
[28] see Draeger and Smith, 1969, p. 35
[29] Yampolsky, 1971, p. 69
[30] see Welch, 1957

❖ Glossary of Terms ❖

arhat [Sanskrit]: A saint who is fully liberated, having achieved *nirvana*.

Ayurveda [Sanskrit]: (lit., the knowledge [science] of [long] life [or health]) An ancient system of healing in India.

Buddhism: A pan-Asian religious tradition dating back some 2500 years associated with Shakyamuni, the Buddha. His teaching consisted of the Four Noble Truths, the last of which was the affirmation of a new way of deliverance from the endless round of birth and dying.

cakra [Sanskrit]: Centers situated proximal to the spinal column in the subtle body, beginning at its base and generally extending to the top of the head that serve as channels of various energies.

Ch'an [Chinese]: In Chinese Buddhism, a general term for meditation. Identifying characteristics of this approach include a special transmission outside of the scriptures, no dependence on words and letters, seeing into one's own nature, and attaining Buddhahood.

Confucianism: A central religious and philosophical tradition of China, also known as the "school of the learned." In this religion, there is no pantheon of gods, creed, or official organization. The importance of ancestor worship and morality (harmony, moderation, filial piety) is stressed.

Dao [Chinese]: A fundamental concept of Chinese thought, indicating broadly the "way," path, or eternal principle. With the Daoists, it became the unity under the plurality of the universe.

Daoism [Chinese]: A collective term used in the West for two different movements of Chinese philosophy, Philosophical Daoism and Religious Doism. The former is a mystical teaching about Dao whereas the various sects of religious Daoism focused on the attainment of immortality.

dharma [Sanskrit]: A broad reference to "religion"; also, the essential

139

foundation of something or things in general; it denotes truth, "correctness" (the way things are or should be), knowledge, morality, and duty.

dhyana [Sanskrit]: A current of unified thought; a continuum of mental efforts to assimilate the object of meditation free from any other effort to assimilate other objects.

Do [Japanese]: "Way"; the path followed in life that, resting upon ethical, philosophical, and spiritual foundations, is expressed through training in a prescribed manner, directed towards an ideal of self-perfection (enlightenment).

gyoja [Japanese]: A Buddhist ascetic.

ida [Sanskrit]: An important *nadi* that plays a role in all Yogic techniques, located to the left of the *susumna*.

kundalini [Sanskrit]: Energy located proximally to the base of the spine that, when aroused through Yogic practices, runs up the *susumna* and upon reaching the top of the head, effects ecstasy and final liberation.

Mahayana [Sanskrit]: A development of thought and practice within Buddhism from the first century that emphasized the supramundane personality of the Buddha as the essence of phenomena, the *bodhisattva* ideal (one destined to become enlightened, a future Buddha) and the philosophy of *sunyata* (void).

mandala [Sanskrit]: A symbolic diagram often comprising a circular border and one or more concentric circles enclosing a square divided into four triangles. Here it is used as a support aid in concentrative meditation.

mantra [Sanskrit]: Any combination of letters believed to be of divine origin and used to evoke divine powers and realize a communion of man with the divine source and essence of the universe.

marman [Sanskrit]: Vulnerable points in the human body.

moksa [Sanskrit]: Final or eternal emancipation; release from worldly existence and the Cycle of death-rebirth in the physical world.

mudra [Sanskrit]: A gesture, finger posture, or symbolic position of the hand used in ritual and meditation.

nadi [Sanskrit]: (lit., conduits, vessels, nerves) The channel through which vital energy circulates throughout the subtle body.

pingala [Sanskrit]: An important *nadi* that plays a role in Yogic techniques, located to the right of the *susumna*.

pratyahara [Sanskrit]: Emancipation of sensory activity from the domination of exterior objects.

qi [Chinese]: (lit., air, vapor, breath, atmosphere) A central concept in Daoism and Chinese medicine. In the Daoist view *qi* is the vital energy, the life-force, the cosmic spirit that pervades and enlivens all things and is therefore synonymous with primordial energy. Also known as *ch'i*.

samadhi [Sanskrit]: In the context used here, a meditative state of consciousness characterized by ecstasy, alert absorption, and unification.

satori [Japanese]: Zen term for the experience of awakening (enlightenment).

sennin [Japanese]: A hermit thought to have magical and supernatural powers.

Shingon [Japanese]: A tantric Buddhist sect introduced to Japan by the priest Kukai in the ninth century that emphasizes reciting *mantras*, rituals, and the practice of meditation especially with the aid of *mandalas*.

Shinto [Japanese]: (lit., Way of the Gods) The original religion of Japan. Early Shinto is characterized by belief in a multitude of deities. Every mountain, every river—all forms of nature are associated with a deity *(kami)*. The most important deities are father Heaven and mother Earth, who created the Japanese islands and the rest of the deities.

shugenja [Japanese]: A monk who leads an ascetic life in the mountains.

Son [Korean]: A form of Buddhism introduced to Korea during the sixth and seventh centuries. By the ninth century, it became an influential movement with the formation and emergence of nine Son sects. Son regards language and ordinary logic as an obstacle to the thought process and stresses the importance of "transcendental intuition."

susumna [Sanskrit]: The central channel or *nadi* of the subtle body located proximal to the spine in the physical body; it plays a significant role in Yogic techniques.

Tendai [Japanese]: A religious tradition introduced to Japan in the ninth century whose philosophical base is the *Lotus Sutra* and that attributes the Buddha-nature to the ordinary man affirming that enlightenment is aided by moralistic ways and rigorous meditation.

Void: A Buddhist concept/experience referring to phenomena seen as empty of self or anything similar; it can also refer to the realization that phenomena are empty of any substantial existence.

yamabushi [Japanese]: A mountain ascetic.

yin-yang [Chinese]: The ancient Chinese theory of the two opposite and complimentary forces in nature. Yin is associated with the feminine, earth, darkness, moon, night, cold, and passivity. Yang is associated with the masculine, heavens, light, heat, day, sun, and activity.

Yoga [Sanskrit]: (lit., Yoke) In Hinduism this has the sense of harnessing oneself to God, seeking union with Him.

Zen [Japanese]: Meditation in the way of the historic Buddha that appeared as a formal practice in Japan in the ninth century. It emphasizes an independence from texts, the experience of enlightenment *(satori)*, and an application of its teachings to daily work and art.

❖ Bibliography ❖

Ackroyd, Joyce. (1987). Bushido. In Mircea Eliade (Ed.), *The Encyclopedia of Religion* (Vol. 2, pp. 581–84). New York: Macmillan.

Agoncillo, Teodoro A., and Alfonso, Oscar M. (1967). *History of the Filipino People*. Quezon City, Philippines: Malaya Books.

Alexander, Howard, Chambers, Quintin, and Draeger, Donn F. (1970). *Pentjak Silat: The Indonesian Fighting Art*. Tokyo, Japan: Kodansha International.

Almeida, Bira. (1981). *Capoeira: A Brazilian Art Form*. Berkeley, California: North Atlantic Press.

Alter, Joseph S. (1992). *The Wrestler's Body: Identity and Ideology in North India*. Berkeley, California: University of California Press.

Amos, Daniel M. (1984). Marginality and the Hero's Art: Martial Artists in Hong Kong and Guangzhou (Canton) (Doctoral Dissertation, University of California, Los Angeles, Department of Anthropology, 1983). *Dissertation Abstracts International, 45*, 227A.

An, Ho-sang. (1977). *Minjok Ai Chuch'esong Kwa Hwarang Ol* [National Self-Consciousness and Hwarangdo]. Seoul: Baeyoung.

An, Kwak. (1974). *Choson Musa Yong'ung Chon* [The Biographies of Korean Martial Artists and Heroes]. Seoul: Chung Um So.

Anuar, Abd. Wahab. (1992). *Teknik Dalam Seni Silat Melayu* [Techniques in Malaysian Martial Arts]. Kuala Lumpur: Dewan Bahasa Dan Pustaka, Kementerian Pendidikan Malaysia.

Armstrong, Hunter B. (1984, December). Jargon in Hoplology. *Hoplos*.

Avalon, Arthur [Woodroffe, Sir John]. (1964). *The Serpent Power, Being Sat-Cakra-Nirupana And Paduka-Pancaka* (7th Ed.). Madras: Ganesh and Company.

Ayukai, Fusanoshin (Ed.). (1931). *Zakko* (Vol. 1). [Studies of miscellanies]. Seoul: Chosen Insatsu Kabushi Kaisha.

143

_____. (1932). *Zakko* (Vol. 4). [Studies of miscellanies]. Seoul: Cho-
sen Insatsu Kabushi Kaisha.

Bakar, Jamil, Esten, Mursal, Surin, Agustar, and Busri. (1981). *Sastra
Lisan Minangkabau: Peptah, Pantum, Dan Mantra* [Oral Literature
of Minankabau: Proverb, Quatrain and Mantra]. Jakarta: Pusat Pem-
binaan Dan Pengembangan Bahasa Departemen Dan Kebudayaan.

Baldrian, Farzeen. (1987). Taoism: An Overview. In Mircea Eliade (Ed.),
The Encyclopedia of Religion (Vol. 14, pp. 288–306). New York:
Macmillan.

Barre, Anton. (1988). Pendak Kendang: Three Dimensions of Indonesian Martial Arts Training Set in a Body-Cultural Perspective.
Centering, (1).

_____. (in preparation). *The Development of Pencak Silat: Body-Cul-
tural Traditions in West Java's Modernization Process in Relation to
Indonesia's Sport- and Culture-Political Strategies.* Unpublished Doctoral Dissertation, University of Copenhagen, Institute of Cultural
Sociology.

Beasley, Jerry. (1983). *The Development of American Karate: History and
Skills.* Greenville, North Carolina: Bemjo Martial Arts Library.

_____. (1989). *In Search of the Ultimate Martial Art: The Jeet Kune Do
Experience.* Boulder, Colorado: Paladin Press.

_____. (1992). *The Way of No Way: Solving the Jeet Kune Do Riddle.*
Boulder, Colorado: Paladin Press.

Becker, Carl B. (1982). Philosophical Perspectives on the Martial Arts
in America. *Journal of the Philosophy of Sport, 9,* 19–29.

Berk, William R. (Ed.). (1979). *Chinese Healing Arts: Internal Kung Fu*
(John Dudgeon, Trans). Culver City, California: Peace Press.

Bharati, Agehananda. (1976). *The Light at the Center.* Santa Barbara:
Ross-Erikson.

Bisio, Thomas. (1983, February). Pencak Silat: The Martial Art of
Indonesia. *Kick Illustrated,* pp. 52–53, 74–75.

Blofeld, John (Trans.). (1962). *Zen Teachings of Hui Hai on Sudden Illumination.* London: Rider.

Borine, Norman. (in press). *King Dragon.* Unpublished Book.

Brocka, J. Cui. (1979). *The Art and Secrets of a Filipino Martial Art:
Philippine Combat Arnis* (Vol. 1). Manila: World Union of Martial
Arts.

Buswell, Robert Evans. (1987). Buddhism In Korea. In Mircea Eliade
(Ed.), *The Encyclopedia of Religion* (Vol. 2, pp. 421–26). New York:
Macmillan.

Buswell, Robert E. and Gimello, Robert M. (1992). *Paths To Liberation: Marga and Its Transformations in Buddhist Thought.* Honolulu, Hawaii: University of Hawaii Press (Series: Kuroda Institute Studies in East Asian Buddhism, No. 7).

Cañete, Ciriaco C., and Cañete, Dionisio A. (1976). *Arnis (Eskrima): Philippines' Stickfighting Art.* Cebu City, Philippines: Doce Pares.

Cauhepe, J. D., and Kuang, A. (1984). *Les Arts Martiaux Interiorises ou L'aikido de la Sagesse* [Internal Martial Arts or the Wisdom of Aikido]. Paris: Editions de la Maisnie.

Chambers, Quintin, and Draeger, Donn F. (1978). *Javanese Silat: The Fighting Art of Perisai Diri.* New York: Kodansha International.

Chan, Wing-tsit (Trans.). (1963). *A Source Book in Chinese Philosophy.* New Jersey: Princeton University Press.

Chattopadhyay, Aparna. (1966–67). Martial Life of Brahmanas in Early Medieval India as Known from the Kathasaritsagara. *Journal of the Oriental Institute, 16,* 52–59.

Chen, Ellen Marie. (1973). Is There a Doctrine of Physical Immortality in the Tao Te Ching? *History of Religions, 12,* 231–49.

Chen, Tsangi-mi (Ed.). (no date). *I-Chin Ching* [Cultivating the Muscles Classic]. Hong Kong: Ch'en Hsiang-Chi Shu-Chu.

Ch'en, I-jen. (1969). *Liu-Ho Pa-Fa Ch'üan.* Hong Kong: Hua-Yu Hsin-Yi Chien-K'ang- She.

Ch'en, Kenneth K.S. (1964). *Buddhism in China: A Historical Survey.* Princeton, New Jersey: Princeton University Press.

Cheng, Man-ch'ing. (1985b). *Cheng Tzu's Thirteen Treatises on T'ai Chi Ch'üan* (Benjamin Pang Jeng Lo and Martin Inn, Trans.). Berkeley: North Atlantic Books.

Cheng, Man-ch'ing and Smith, Robert W. (1967). *Tai Chi: The "Supreme Ultimate" Exercise for Health, Sport, and Self-Defense.* Tokyo, Japan: Charles E. Tuttle.

Cheung, William. (1983). *Wing Chun Bil Jee.* Hollywood, California: Unique.

_____. (1985). *Wing Chun Advanced Chi Sao and Applications.* Hollywood, California: Unique.

Cheung, William, and Wong, Ted. (1990). *Wing Chun Kung Fu/Jeet Kune Do: A Comparison* (Vol. 1). Santa Clarita, California: Ohara.

Chinul. (1983). *The Korean Approach to Zen: The Collected Works of Chinul* (Robert E. Buswell, Trans.). Honolulu, Hawaii: University of Hawaii Press.

Chow, Christopher Hsin-Ren. (1959). *A Metaphysical Inquiry Into the*

Ultimate Incomprehensibility of Tao. Unpublished Bachelor's Thesis, University of Chicago, Divinity School.

Chow, David, and Spangler, Richard. (1977). *Kung Fu: Philosophy and Technique*. Garden City, New York: Doubleday.

Chuang Tzu. (1968). *The Complete Works of Chuang-Tzu* (Burton Watson, Trans.). New York: Columbia University Press.

Chung, Sun Hwan. (1979). *Oriental Martial Arts*. Korea: N.P.

Clark, E. Culpepper, Hyde, Michael J., and McMahan, Eva M. (1980). Communication in the Oral History Interview: Investigating Problems of Interpreting Oral Data. *International Journal of Oral History*, *1*, 28–40.

Clouse, Robert. (1987). *The Making of Enter the Dragon*. Burbank, California: Unique.

————. (1988). *Bruce Lee: The Biography*. Burbank, California: Unique.

Co, Alexander (Ed. and Trans.). (1983). *The Way of Ngo Cho Kun Kung Fu*. Manila, Philippines: Jafaha Publications.

————. (1983, October). White Crane: Secrets of Three Styles. *Inside Kung Fu*, pp. 48–52.

Colberg, Fran. (1975a, May). Taido . . . Japan's Martial Art of the Future. *Karate Illustrated*, pp. 18–20, 39–45.

Colet, Robert. (1986, August). Krishnamurti: The Spiritual Force Behind Bruce Lee. *Inside Kung Fu*, pp. 73–75.

Collcutt, Martin. (1981). *Five Mountains: The Rinzai Zen Monastic Institution in Medieval Japan*. Cambridge: Harvard University Press.

Conze, Edward. (1953). The Ontology of the Prajña-Paramita. *Philosophy East And West*, *3* (2), 117–29.

————. (1959). *Buddhism: Its Essence and Development*. New York: Harper and Row.

Cook, Francis H. (1983). Enlightenment in Dogen's Zen. *Journal of the International Association of Buddhist Studies*, *6* (1), 7–30.

Corcoran, John, and Farkas, Emil. (1983). *Martial Arts: Traditions, History, People*. New York: Gallery Books.

Cordes, Hiltrud T. (1990). *Pencak Silat: Die Kampfkunst der Minangkabau und Ihr Kulturelles Umfeld* [Pencak Silat: The Fighting Art of the Minangkabau People and their Cultural Environment]. Unpublished Doctoral Dissertation, University of Köln, Department of Cultural Anthropology, Faculty of Philosophy.

Crim, Keith, Bullard, Roger A., and Shinn, Larry D. (1981). *Abingdon Dictionary of Living Religions*. Nashville, Tennessee: Abingdon.

D'Aquino, Iria. (1983). Capoeira: Strategies for Status, Power and

Identity (Doctoral Dissertation, University of Illinois, Champaign-Urbana). *Dissertation Abstracts International, 44,* 1850a.

Dann, Jeffrey Lewis. (1978). "Kendo" In Japanese Martial Culture: Swordsmanship as Self-Cultivation (Doctoral Dissertation, University of Washington, Department of Anthropology). *Dissertation Abstracts International, 39,* 960A.

David Manuel Raj, J. (1971). *Silambam: Technique and Evaluation.* Karaikudi: Higginbothams.

Demiéville, Paul. (1957). Le Bouddhisme et la Guerre [Buddhism and War]. *Melanges Publiés par l'institut des Hautes Études Chinoises, 1,* 347–85.

_____. (1952). *Le Concile de Lhasa: Une Controverse sur le Quietisme Entre Bouddhistes de l'Inde et de la Chine au Viiie Siecle de l'ère Chré Tienne* [The Council of Lhasa: A Controversy on Quietism Between Buddhists of India and China in the 8th Century of the Christian Era]. Paris: Presses Universitaires de France. (Series: Bibliotheque de l'institut des Hautes Etudes Chinoises, Vol. 7).

DeMile, James W. (1977). *Tao of Wing Chun Do: Mind and Body in Harmony.* Santa Rosa, California: Tao of Wing Chun Do.

_____. (1978a). *Bruce Lee's Chi Sao* (Sticking Hands). (Tao of Wing Chun Do, Vol. 2). Santa Rosa, California: Tao of Wing Chun Do.

Deshimaru, Taisen. (1982). *The Zen Way to the Martial Arts.* New York: E. P. Dutton.

Deshpande, S.H. (no date). *Religio-Philosophical Basis of Physical Education in Indian Culture.* Unpublished Manuscript.

Despeux, Catherine. (1975). *T'ai-Ki K'iuan, Technique de Longue Vie, Technique de Combat* [Taijiquan, Technique of Long Life, Technique of Combat]. Paris: College De France. (Series: Mémoires de l'institut des Hautes Études Chinoises, Vol. 3).

Donohue, John J. (1991). *The Forge of the Spirit: Structure, Motion and Meaning in the Japanese Martial Tradition.* New York: Garland.

Draeger, Donn F. (1972). *Weapons and Martial Arts of the Indonesian Archipelago.* Tokyo: Charles E. Tuttle.

_____. (1973a). *Classical Bujutsu: The Martial Arts and Ways of Japan* (Vol. 1). New York: Weatherhill.

_____. (1973b). *Classical Budo: The Martial Arts and Ways of Japan* (Vol. 2). New York: Weatherhill.

_____. (1974a). Japanese Martial Arts and Ways: Part 1. The Japanese Martial Arts are Different from the Japanese Martial Ways. *Martial Arts International, 1*(1), 7–8.

_____. (1974b). *Modern Bujutsu and Budo: The Martial Arts and Ways of Japan* (Vol. 3). New York: Weatherhill.

_____. (1977). *Classical Hawaiian Martial Culture*. Unpublished Manuscript.

_____. (1980a, September). Let Me Count the Ways: Part III. *Hoplos, 2–3*.

_____. (1980b). The Martial Arts: An Inside View. In 1980 *Britannica Book of the Year* (pp. 255–56). Chicago: Encyclopedia Britannica.

_____. (1981b, February). The Martial-Civil Dichotomy in Asian Combatives. *Hoplos*, p. 6–8.

Draeger, Donn, Kiong, Tjoa-Khak, and Chambers, Quintin. (1976). *Shantung Black Tiger: A Shaolin Fighting Art of North China*. New York: Weatherhill.

Draeger, Donn, and Leong, Cheong-Cheng. (1977). *Phoenix-Eye Fist: A Shaolin Fighting Art of South China*. New York: Weatherhill.

Draeger, Donn F., and Smith, Robert W. (1969). *Comprehensive Asian Martial Arts*. Tokyo, Japan: Kodansha International.

Dumoulin, Heinrich. (1951). Bodhidharma und die Anfange des Ch'an-Buddhismus [Bodhidharma and the Beginnings of Ch'an Buddhism]. *Monumenta Nipponica, 7*, 67–83.

Dumoulin, Heinrich. (1953). *The Development of Chinese Zen After the Sixth Patriarch in the Light of Mumonkan*. New York: First Zen Institute of America.

Earhart, H. Byron. (1987). Shugendo. In Mircea Eliade (Ed.), *The Encyclopedia of Religion* (Vol. 13, pp. 302–5). New York: Macmillan.

Egerton, Wilbraham Egerton. (1968). *Indian and Oriental Armour*. London: Arms and Armour Press.

Eliade, Mircea. (1969). *Yoga: Immortality and Freedom* (2nd Ed.). Princeton: Princeton University Press.

_____. (1982). *A History of Religious Ideas* (Vol. 2). Chicago: University of Chicago Press.

Engelhardt, Ute. (1987). *Die Klassische Tradition der Qi-Bungen (Qigong): Eine Darstellung Anhand des Tang-Zeitlichen Textes Fuqi Jingyi Lun von Sima Chengzhen* [The Classical Tradition of Qigong: A Demonstration According to Texts of the Tang Period, Thesis on the Essential Meaning of Absorbing Qi by Sima Chengzhen]. Stuttgart: F. Steiner Verlag Wiesbaden. (Series: Munchener Ostasiatische Studien, 0170-3668; Bd. 44)

Esnoul, A. M. (1987). Moksa. In Mircea Eliade (Ed.), *The Encyclopedia of Religion* (Vol. 9, pp. 224–28). New York: Macmillan.

Evleshin, Catherine. (1986). Capoeira at the Crossroads. *UCLA Journal of Dance Ethnology, 10,* 7–17.

Farquhar, J. N. (1925). The Fighting Ascetics of India. *Bulletin of the John Rylands Library, 9,* 431–52.

Farris, William Wayne. (1993). *Heavenly Warriors: The Evolution of Japan's Military, 500–1300.* Cambridge: Harvard University Press.

Felipe, Nemesio Marcelo. (1926). *A Historical Study of Pre-Christian Philippine Morality.* Unpublished Master's Thesis, University of Chicago, Department of Philosophy.

Feuerstein, Georg. (1987). Samadhi. In Mircea Eliade (Ed.), *The Encyclopedia of Religion* (Vol. 13, pp. 32–33). New York: Macmillan.

Fischer, Herbert. (1963). Indogermanischer Kriegeryoga [Indo-European Warrior Yoga]. In Hans Riehl (Ed.), *Festschrift Walter Heinrich* (pp. 65–97). Graz- Austria: Akademische Druck-u. Verlagsanstalt.

Fong, Leo T. (1976). *Wei Kune Do: The Psychodynamic Art of Free Fighting.* Stockton, California: Koinonia Publications.

————. (1986). *Modified Wing Chun Kung Fu: Theory and Concepts* (Vol. 1). Englewood, Colorado: Action Communications, Inc.

Foronda, Marcelino A., Jr. (1981). Oral History in the Philippines: Trends and Projects. *International Journal of Oral History, 2* (1), 13–25.

Friday, Karl F. (1992). *Hired Swords: The Rise of Private Power in Early Japan.* Stanford, California: Stanford University Press.

Gilbey, John F. (1982). *The Way of a Warrior.* Richmond, California: North Atlantic Books.

Glover, Jesse. (1976). *Bruce Lee: Between Wing Chun and Jeet Kune Do.* Seattle, Washington: Glover Publications.

————. (1981). *Non-Classical Gung Fu.* Seattle, Washington: Glover Publications.

Gluck, Jay. (1962). *Zen Combat.* New York: Ballantine Books.

Gorn, Elliott Jacob. (1984). The Manly Art: Bare-Knuckle Prize Fighting and the Rise of American Sports (Doctoral Dissertation, Yale University, 1983). *Dissertation Abstracts International, 44,* 2808A.

Gregory, Peter N. (Ed.). (1987a). *Sudden and Gradual: Approaches to Enlightenment in Chinese Thought.* Honolulu, Hawaii: University of Hawaii Press (Series: Kuroda Institute Studies in East Asian Buddhism, No. 5).

Gregory, Peter N. (1987b). Sudden Enlightenment Followed by Gradual Cultivation: Tsung-Mi's Analysis of Mind. In Peter N. Gregory (Ed.), *Sudden and Gradual: Approaches to Enlightenment in Chinese Thought*. Honolulu, Hawaii: University of Hawaii Press (Series: Kuroda Institute Studies in East Asian Buddhism, No. 5).

_____. (1991). *Tsung-Mi and the Sinification of Buddhism*. New Jersey: Princeton University Press.

Haines, Bruce A. (1995). *Karate's History and Traditions (Revised Edition)*. Tokyo, Japan: Charles E. Tuttle.

Hall, David A. (1979a, November). Bu-jutsu and the Esoteric Tradition: Part I of II. *Hoplos*, pp. 1–4.

_____. (1979b, December). Bu-jutsu and the Esoteric Tradition: Part II of II. *Hoplos*, pp. 2–5, 7.

_____. (1989). Martial Aspects of the Buddhist Marici in Sixth Century China. *Annual of the Institute for Comprehensive Studies of Buddhism, Taisho University*, 11, 199–182.

_____. (1990). Marishiten: Buddhism and the Warrior Goddess. (Doctoral Dissertation, University of California, Berkeley, Department of Buddhist Studies). *Dissertation Abstracts International*, 51, 3109A.

Hallander, Jane. (1984). The Hand as a Sword: Korean Steel Palm Training. *Karate Illustrated: The 1984 Yearbook*, pp. 28–32.

Harrison, Ernest John. (1966). *The Fighting Spirit of Japan*. New York: Foulsham.

Hartsell, Larry. (1984). *Jeet Kune Do: Entering to Trapping to Grappling*. Burbank, California: Unique.

Hartsell, Larry, and Tackett, Tim. (1987). *Jeet Kune Do, Volume 2: Counterattack! Grappling Counters and Reversals*. Burbank, California: Unique.

Hatada, Takashi. (1951). *Chosen-Shi* [History of Korea]. Tokyo: Iwanami Shoten.

Hatsumi, Masaaki. (1981b). *Nin-jutsu: History and Tradition*. Hollywood, California: Unique.

Hayes, Stephen K. (1980). *Ninja: Spirit of the Shadow Warrior (Vol. 1)*. Burbank, California: Ohara.

Hayes, Stephen K. (1981a). *Ninja: Warrior Ways of Enlightenment (Vol. 2)*. Burbank, California: Ohara.

_____. (1981b). *The Ninja and their Secret Fighting Art*. Tokyo, Japan: Charles E. Tuttle.

_____. (1985). *The Mystic Arts of the Ninja: Hypnotism, Invisibility and Weaponry*. Chicago: Contemporary.

Henning, Stanley E. (1981). The Chinese Martial Arts in Historical Perspective. *Military Affairs, 45* (4), 173–78.

Henthorn, William E. (1971). A History of Korea. New York: The Free Press.

Herrigel, Eugen. (1953). *Zen in the Art of Archery.* New York: Pantheon Books.

Hirai, Naofusa. (1987). Shinto. In Mircea Eliade (Ed.), *The Encyclopedia of Religion* (Vol. 13, pp. 280–94). New York: Macmillan.

Hosillos, Lucila V. (1969). *Philippine-American Literary Relations 1898–1941.* Quezon City: University of the Philippines Press.

Huang, Wen-shan. (1974). *Fundamentals of Tai Chi Ch'üan* (2nd Ed.). Hong Kong: South Sky Book Company.

Huard, Pierre, and Wong, Ming. (1977). *Oriental Methods of Mental and Physical Fitness: The Complete Book of Meditation, Kinesitherapy and Martial Arts in China, India and Japan.* New York: Funk and Wagnells.

Hurst, G. Cameron. (1990). Death, Honor, and Loyalty: The Bushido Ideal. *Philosophy East And West, 40* (4), 511–27.

_____. (1993). From Heiho to Bugei: The Emergence of the Martial Arts in Tokugawa Japan. *Journal of Asian Martial Arts, 2* (4), 40–51.

_____. (in press). *The Martial Arts of Japan, Volume 1: Swordsmanship and Archery.* New Haven: Yale University Press.

Hyams, Joe. (1979). *Zen in the Martial Arts.* Los Angeles: J. P. Tarcher.

Ilyon. (1972). *Samguk Yusa* [Legends of the Three Kingdoms] (Tae-Hung Ha and Graften K. Mintz, Trans.). Seoul: Yonsei University Press.

Inosanto, Dan. (1976). *Jeet Kune Do: The Art and Philosophy of Bruce Lee.* Los Angeles, California: Know Now.

_____. (1980a). *A Guide to Martial Arts Training with Equipment: A Jeet Kune Do Guidebook (Vol. 1).* Los Angeles, California: Know Now.

_____. (1980b). *The Filipino Martial Arts.* Los Angeles, California: Know Now.

_____. (1982). *Absorb What Is Useful: A Jeet Kune Do Guidebook (Vol. 2).* Los Angeles, California: Know Now.

_____. (1986b, August). JKD: What's in a Name? *Inside Kung Fu,* pp. 14, 16, 32.

Johnson, Jerry Alan. (1984). *The Masters Manual of Pa Kua Chang.* Pacific Grove, California: Ching Lung Martial Arts Association, Inc.

Jones, Halford E. (1983, September). Secrets of Silat. *Kick Illustrated,* pp. 61–63.

Kalb, Ben. (1977, August). The Transformation of a Cosmic Oatmeal Cookie to Black Belt. *Karate Illustrated,* pp. 46–47.

Kammer, Reinhard. (1978). *Zen and Confucius in the Art of Swordsmanship: The Tengu-Gei-jutsu-Ron of Chozan Shissai* (Betty J. Fitzgerald, Trans.). London: Routledge and Kegan Paul.

Kasulis, Thomas P. (1987). Nirvana. In Mircea Eliade (Ed.), *The Encyclopedia of Religion* (Vol. 10, pp. 448–56). New York: Macmillan.

Keeley, Liam. (1986, spring). Zulu Stickfighting. *Hoplos,* 1–12.

Kent, Chris, and Tackett, Tim. (1986). *Jeet Kune Do Kickboxing.* Los Angeles, California: Know Now.

————. (1988). *Jun Fan/Jeet Kune Do: The Textbook.* Los Angeles, California: Know Now.

Kim, Chang Sik, and Kim, Maria. (1985). *The Art of Zen Sword: The History of Shim Gum Do (Part 1).* Brighton, Massachusetts: American Buddhist Shim Gum Do Association.

Kim, Chong Sun. (1961). *Hwarang and the First Unification of Korea.* Unpublished Master's Thesis, University of Washington, Department of Far Eastern Studies.

Kim, Chong Sun. (1966). The Emergence of Multi-Centered Despotism in the Silla Kingdom: A Study of the Origin of Factional Struggles in Korea (Doctoral Dissertation, University of Washington, Department of Far Eastern Studies, 1965). *Dissertation Abstracts International, 27,* 427A–428A.

Kim, Haboush, JaHyun. (1987). Confucianism in Korea. In Mircea Eliade (Ed.), *The Encyclopedia of Religion* (Vol. 4, pp. 10–15). New York: Macmillan.

Kim, Pu-Sik. (1931). *Samguk Sagi* [History of Three Kingdoms] (Koten Kankokai, Trans.). Seoul: Kotan Kankokai.

King, Winston L. (1986). *Death Was His Koan: The Samurai-Zen of Suzuki Shosan.* Berkeley: Asian Humanities Press. (Series: Nanzan Studies in Religion and Culture, No. 5).

————. (1992). *Zen And the Way of the Sword.* New York: Oxford.

Kitagawa, Joseph M. (1981). The Career of Maitreya, with Special Reference to Japan. *History of Religions, 21* (2), 107–25.

Kiyota, Minoru. (1978b). *Shingon Buddhism: Theory and Practice.* Los Angeles: Buddhist Books International.

————. (1990). Buddhist Thought in Kendo And Bushido: The Ten-shin Shoden School of Swordsmanship. In Minoru Kiyota and Hideaki Kinoshita (Eds.), *Japanese Martial Arts and American Sports: Cross-Cultural Perspectives on Means to Personal Growth* (pp. 17–28). Tokyo: Nihon University Press.

_____. (1990). *Japanese Martial Arts and American Sports: Cross-Cultural Perspectives on Means to Personal Growth*. Tokyo: Nihon University Press.

Koesnoen, A. (1963). *Pentjak Silat*. Bandung, Sumur Bandung.

Koh, T.C. (1981). Tai Chi Chuan. *American Journal of Chinese Medicine, 9* (1), 15–22.

Kondo, Hitoshi. (1978). *Sengoku Jidai Buke Kakun Kenkyu* [Studies on Family Precepts for Warriors in the Age of the Warring States]. Tokyo: Kazama Shobo.

Kraitus, Panya, and Kraitus, Dr. Pitisuk. (1988). *Muay Thai: The Most Distinguished Art of Fighting*. Phuket, Thailand: Author.

Krieger, Herbert W. (1926). The Collection of Primitive Weapons and Armor of the Philippine Islands In the United States National Museum. *Bulletin, Smithsonian Institution, No. 137*.

_____. (1942). Peoples of the Philippines. *Smithsonian Institution War Background Studies, No. 4*.

Kroeber, A. L. (1918). The History of Philippine Civilization as Reflected In Religious Nomenclature. *Anthropological Papers of the American Museum of Natural History, 19* (2), 35–67.

Lancaster, Lewis R. (1987). Maitreya. In Mircea Eliade (Ed.), *The Encyclopedia of Religion* (Vol. 9, pp. 136–41). New York: Macmillan.

Lancaster, Lewis. (1988). Maitreya in Korea. In Alan Sponberg and Helen Hardacre (Eds.), *Maitreya, the Future Buddha* (pp. 135–53). New York: Cambridge University Press.

Lao Tzu. (1963). *Tao Te Ching* [The Way and Its Power] (D. L. Lau, Trans.). Baltimore: Penguin.

Lau, Jim (Ed.). (1981). *The World of Bruce Lee*. Hong Kong: The World of Bruce Lee Hong Kong Publications.

Lee, Bruce. (1963). *Chinese Gung Fu: The Philosophical Art of Self Defense*. Oakland, California: Oriental Book Sales.

_____. (1969). The "Chi Sao" of Wing Chun. *Black Belt: The 1969 Yearbook*, pp. 25–32.

_____. (1970). Foreword. In Stirling Silliphant, *The Silent Flute* (pp. IV–V). n.p.: Pingree-Panpiper Productions.

_____. (1975). *Tao of Jeet Kune Do*. Burbank, California: Ohara.

_____. (1986). Liberate Yourself from Classical Karate. In Black Belt Magazine (Eds.), *The Legendary Bruce Lee* (pp. 62–69). Burbank, California: Ohara. (Original work published 1971 [September, Black Belt]).

Lee, Greglon, and Campbell, Sid. (in press). *Dragon and Tiger: The Oakland Years*. Foster City, California: Crocker-Edwards Publishing Company.

Lee, James Y. (1972). *Wing Chun Kung Fu*. Burbank, California: Ohara.

Lee, Joo Bang. (1978). *The Ancient Martial Art of Hwarang Do*. Burbank, California: Ohara.

Lee, Joo Bang. (1979). *The Ancient Martial Art of Hwarang Do (Vol. 2)*. Burbank, California: Ohara.

_____. (1980). *The Ancient Martial Art of Hwarang Do (Vol. 3)*. Burbank, California: Ohara.

Lee, Linda. (1975). *Bruce Lee: The Man Only I Knew*. New York: Warner.

Lee, Linda, and Bleecker, Tom. (1989). *The Bruce Lee Story*. Burbank, California: Ohara.

Leggett, Trevor. (1978). *Zen and the Ways*. Boulder, Colorado: Shambala.

_____. (1985). *The Warrior Koans: Early Zen in Japan*. Boston: Arkana.

Leung, Ting. (1978). *Wing Tsun Kuen*. Hong Kong: International Wing Tsun Leung Ting Martial Arts Association.

Levi, Sylvain. (1932). Maitreya le Consolateur [Maitreya the Consoler]. *Etudes d'Orientalisme, Tome II*, 355–402.

Levi, Sylvain, and Chavannes, Edouard. (1916). Les Seize Arhat Protecteurs de la Loi [The Sixteen Arhat Protectors of the Law]. *Journal Asiatique, 8 (Series 2)*, 5–50, 189–304.

Lewis, John Lowell. (1986). Semeiotic and Social Discourse In Brazilian Capoeira. (Doctoral Dissertation, University of Washington, Department of Anthropology). *Dissertation Abstracts International, 48*, 426A.

_____. (1992). *Ring of Liberation: Deceptive Discourse in Brazilian Capoeira*. Chicago: University of Chicago Press.

Liang, T. T. (1977). *T'ai Chi Ch'uan for Health and Self-Defense: Philosophy and Practice*. New York: Vintage.

Lineberger, Pat. (1988, Fall). A Radio Interview with Donn F. Draeger, Part II. *Hoplos*, 18–25.

Lorenzen, David N. (1978). Warrior Ascetics in Indian History. *Journal of the American Oriental Society, 98* (1), 61–75.

Maisel, Edward. (1974). *T'ai Chi For Health.* New York: Delta.

Major, John S. (1987a). Ch'i. In Mircea Eliade (Ed.), *The Encyclopedia of Religion* (Vol. 3, pp. 238–39). New York: Macmillan.

_____. (1987b). Yin-Yang Wu-Hsing. In Mircea Eliade (Ed.), *The Encyclopedia of Religion* (Vol. 15, pp. 515–16). New York: Macmillan.

Maliszewski, Michael. (1987). Martial Arts: An Overview. In Mircea Eliade (Ed.), *The Encyclopedia of Religion* (Vol. 9, pp. 224–28). New York: Macmillan.

Maliszewski, Michael. (1990). Injuries in Boxing: Evaluation and Policy Decisions. *The Sport Psychologist, 4,* 55–62.

_____. (1992-a). Injuries and Effects of Martial Arts: A Review. *Journal of Asian Martial Arts, 1* (2), 16–23.

_____. (1992-b). Medical, Healing and Spiritual Components of Asian Martial Arts: A Preliminary Field Study Exploration. *Journal of Asian Martial Arts, 1* (2), 24–57.

_____. (1992-c). Meditative-Religious Traditions of Martial Arts and Martial Ways. *Journal of Asian Martial Arts, 1* (3), 1–104.

_____. (in preparation-a). *A Phenomenological and Comparative Analytic Appraisal of Shaktipat Initiation from the Standpoint of Initiator and Recipient (With Additional Reference to the Kundalini Phenomenon).* Unpublished paper.

Maliszewski, Michael, Twemlow, Stuart, W., Brown, Daniel P., and Engler, John M. (1981). A Phenomenological Typology of Intensive Meditation. *Revision, 4* (2), 3–27.

Mangkunagara VII of Surakarta, K.G.P.A.A. (1957). *On the Wayang Kulit (Purwa) and Its Symbolic and Mystical Elements* (Claire Holt, Trans.) (Data Paper, No. 27). Ithaca, New York: Cornell University, Southeast Asia Program, Department of Far Eastern Studies.

Mañjusrimitra (1986). *Primordial Experience: An Introduction to Dzog-Chen Meditation* (Namkhai Norbu and Kennard Lipman, Trans.). Boston: Shambala.

Mark, Bow-Sim. (1981). *Wushu: Basic Training.* Boston: Chinese Wushu Research Institute.

Maslak, Paul. (1979, November). Was Bruce Lee a Chop-Suey Martial Artist? *Inside Kung-Fu,* pp. 16–19.

Maspero, Henri. (1981a). Methods of "Nourishing the Vital Principle" in the Ancient Taoist Religion. In Henri Maspero, *Taoism and Chi-*

nese Religion (Book 9, pp. 443–54; Frank A. Kierman, Trans.). Amherst: University of Massachusetts Press.

Mass, Jeffrey, P. and Hauser, William B. (Eds.) (1985). *The Bakufu in Japanese History*. Stanford, California: Stanford University Press.

Masui, Jacques (Ed.). (1969). *Le Vide, Experience Spirituelle en Occident et en Orient* [The Void, Spiritual Experience in the West and East]. Paris: Hermes. (Series: Hermes; Recherches sur l'Experience Spirituelle, Vol. 6).

Masunaga, Reiho. (1972). Bodhidharma. In G.P. Malalasekera (Ed.), *Encyclopedia of Buddhism* (Vol. 3, Fascicle 2; pp. 191–99). Ceylon: Government of Ceylon.

Mikisuburi, Mori. (1972). Chuang Tzu And Buddhism. *The Eastern Buddhist, New Series, 5* (2), 44–69.

Mikisuburi, Mori, and Fukunaga, Mitsuji. (1969). "No Mind" in Chuang-Tzu and in Chan Buddhism. *Zinbun, 12,* 9–45.

Miller, Chris. (1990). Ram Muay—Inner Strength. In Patrick Cusick (Ed.), *Muay Thai,* (Vol. 1; pp. 24–29). Bangkok, Thailand: Artasia Press.

Mishina, Shoei. (1934a). Shiragi Karo no Genryu to Sono Hatten [Foundations and Development of Hwarang in Silla] (Pt. 1). *Shigaku Zasshi, 45* (10), 1151–1212.

_____. (1934b). Shiragi Karo no Genryu to Sono Hatten [Foundations and Development of Hwarang in Silla] (Pt. 2). *Shigaku Zasshi, 45* (11), 1313–65.

_____. (1934c). Shiragi Karo no Genryu to Sono Hatten [Foundations and Development of Hwarang in Silla] (Pt. 3). *Shigaku Zasshi, 45* (12), 1465–1512.

Mo, Yon-ho. (1978). *Hwarangdo wa Hwarang Yolchon* [Hwarangdo and Collected Biographies of the Hwarang]. Seoul: Hak Moon.

Moertono, Soemarsaid. (1968). *State and Statecraft in Old Java: A Study of the Later Mataram Period, 16th to 19th Century*. Ithaca, New York: Cornell Southeast Asia Program.

Mogul, Jerry. (1980a). T'ai Chi Ch'uan: A Taoist Art of Healing (Pt. 1). *Somatics, 2* (4), 36–45.

_____. (1980b). T'ai Chi Ch'uan: A Taoist Art of Healing (Pt. 2). *Somatics, 3* (1), 42–49.

Mujumdar, Dattatraya C. (Ed.). (1950). *Encyclopedia of Indian Physical Culture*. Baroda, India: Good Companion.

Mulder, Niels. (1970). A Comparative Note on the Thai and the Javanese Worldview as Expressed by Religious Practice and Belief. *Journal of the Siam Society, 58* (2), 79–85.

_____. (1982). Abangan Javanese Religious Thought and Practice. *Bijdragen Tot de Taal-, Land- en Volkenkunde, 139,* 260–67.

_____. (1983). *Mysticism and Everyday Life in Contemporary Java* (3rd Ed.). Singapore: Singapore University Press.

Murayama, Chijun. (1932). *Chosen no Fugeki* [Shamans of Korea]. Seoul: Chosen Sotoku-Fu.

Mustaffa, Ku Ahmad Bin Ku, and Wong, Kiew Kit. (1978). *Silat Melayu: The Malay Art of Attack and Defence.* Kuala Lumpur, Malaysia: Oxford University Press.

Myers, Thomas I., and Eisner, Ellen J. (1974). *An Experimental Evaluation of the Effects of Karate and Meditation* (Contract No. Dahc 19-74-C-0012). Washington, D.C.: American Institutes for Research.

Nabor, Artemio. (1956). A History of Akean. *Aklan: Journal Devoted to Rural Progress* (Inaugural Number And Souvenir Book).

Nagamine, Shoshin. (1976). *The Essence of Okinawan Karate-Do (Shorin-Ryu).* Tokyo, Japan: Charles E. Tuttle.

Nagashima, Takayuki Shono. (1978). *Truths and Fabrications in Religion: An Investigation from the Documents of the Zen (Ch'an) Sect.* London: Arthur Probsthain.

Needham, Joseph. (1956). *Science and Civilization in China (Vol. 2).* Cambridge: Cambridge University Press.

Nelson, Randy F. (1988). *The Martial Arts: An Annotated Bibliography.* New York: Garland.

Nitobe, Inazo. (1969). *Bushido: The Warrior's Code* (2nd Printing). Burbank, California: Ohara.

Nivison, David S. (1987). Tao and Te. In Mircea Eliade (Ed.), *The Encyclopedia of Religion* (Vol. 14, 283–86). New York: Macmillan.

Norbu, Namkhai. (1986). *The Crystal and the Way of Light: Meditation, Contemplation and Self-Liberation.* New York: Methuen.

_____. (1987a). *Dzog Chen and Zen.* Nevada City, California: Blue Dolphin Press.

_____. (1987b). *The Cycle of Day and Night- Where One Proceeds Along the Path of the Primordial Yoga: A Basic Tibetan Text on the Practice of Dzogchen.* Barrytown, New York: Station Hill Press Inc.

Nosco, Peter. (1987). Confucianism In Japan. In Mircea Eliade (Ed.), *The Encyclopedia of Religion* (Vol. 4, pp. 7–10). New York: Macmillan.

O'Connor, Stanley. (1975). Iron Working as Spiritual Inquiry in the Indonesian Archipelago. *History of Religions, 14* (3), 173–90.

Omari, Mikelle Smith. (1984). *From the Inside to the Outside: The Art and Ritual of Bahian Candomble.* Los Angeles: UCLA Museum of Cultural History. (Series: Museum of Cultural History, UCLA Monograph Series, No. 24).

Omori, Sogen. (1966). *Ken to Zen* [The Sword and Zen]. Tokyo: Shungu.

Onuma, H. DeProspero, D., and DeProspero, J. (1993). *Kyudo: The Essence and Practice of Japanese Archery.* Tokyo: Kodansha.

Orr, W.G. (1940). Armed Religious Ascetics in Northern India. *Bulletin of the John Rylands Library, 24,* 81–100.

Oyama, Masutatsu. (1979). *The Kyokushin Way.* Tokyo: Japan Publications.

Pachow, W. (1972). Bodhidharma. In G.P. Malasekera (Ed.), *Encyclopedia of Buddhism* (Vol. 3, Fascicle 2, pp. 200–5). Ceylon: Government of Ceylon.

Padoux, Andre. (1987). Cakras. In Mircea Eliade (Ed.), *The Encyclopedia of Religion* (Vol. 3, pp. 4–5). New York: Macmillan.

Pant, Gayatri Nash. (1970). *Studies in Indian Weapons and Warfare.* New Delhi: Army Educational Stores.

_____. (1978). *Indian Archery.* Delhi: Agam Kala Prakashan.

Park, Sung Bae. (1980). Korean Monk Chinul's Theory of Sudden Enlightenment. *Asian Culture Quarterly, 8* (4), 12–18.

_____. (1983). *Buddhist Faith and Sudden Enlightenment.* Albany: State University of New York.

Paul, William Wayne. (1980). Aggression, Control, and Nonverbal Communication: Aspects of Asian Martial Arts (Doctoral Dissertation, Harvard University, 1979). *Dissertation Abstracts International, 40,* 5873B.

Payne, Peter. (1981). *Martial Arts: The Spiritual Dimension.* New York: Crossroad.

Presas, Remy Amador. (1974). *Modern Arnis: Philippine Martial Art.* Manila, Philippines: Modern Arnis.

Protin, Andre. (1977). *Aikido: Un Art Martial, une Autre Maniere d'être* [Aikido: A Martial Art, Another Mode of Existence]. St. Jean De Braye: Editions Dangles.

Quick, John. (1973). *A Dictionary of Weapons and Military Terms.* New York: McGraw-Hill.

Raboteau, Albert J. (1987). Afro-Brazilian Cults. In Mircea Eliade (Ed.),

The Encyclopedia of Religion (Vol. 1, pp. 102–5). New York: Macmillan.

Ratti, Oscar, and Westbrook, Adele. (1973). *Secrets of the Samurai: A Survey of the Martial Arts of Feudal Japan*. Tokyo, Japan: Charles E. Tuttle.

Rausa-Gomez, Lourdes. (1967). Sri-Vijaya and Madjapahit. *Philippine Studies, 15* (1), 63–107.

Rego, Waldeloir. (1968). *Capoeira Angola: Ensaio Socio-Ethnografico* [Capoeira of Angola: A Socioethnographic Treatise]. Salvador, Bahia: Editora Itapua.

Reid, Howard, and Croucher, Michael. (1983). *The Martial Arts: Great Masters of the Martial Arts*. New York: Simon and Schuster.

Richards, J. (1982). Conditioning for Judo, and Judo as a Conditioner for Other Sports. *National Strength and Conditioning Association Journal, 4* (1), 32–33, 60.

Riebel, Linda. (1982). Theory as Self-Portrait and the Ideal of Objectivity. *Journal of Humanistic Psychology, 22* (2), 91–110.

Rosu, Arion. (1981). Les Marman et les Arts Martiaux Indiens [The Marman and Indian Martial Arts]. *Journal Asiatique, 269,* 417–51.

Rutt, Richard. (1961). The Flower Boys of Silla (Hwarang): Notes on the Sources. *Transactions of the Korea Branch of the Royal Asiatic Society, 38,* 1–66.

Sammons, Jeffrey Thomas. (1982). America in the Ring: The Relationship Between Boxing and Society Circa 1930–80 (Doctoral Dissertation, University of North Carolina at Chapel Hill). *Dissertation Abstracts International, 43,* 1656A.

Sasaki, Ruth Fuller (Trans.). (1975). *The Recorded Sayings of Ch'an Master Lin-Chi Hui-Chao of Chen Prefecture*. Kyoto, Japan: The Institute for Zen Studies.

Satprem. (1968). *Sri Aurobindo, or The Adventure of Consciousness*. New York: Harper and Row.

Saunders, E. Dale. (1960). *Mudra: A Study of Symbolic Gestures in Japanese Buddhist Sculpture*. London: Routledge and Kegan Paul, Ltd.

Savanta, Abaji Ramacandra. (1914). *Mallavidyaprakasa* [Light of Wrestling Knowledge]. N.P.: Author.

Schipper, Kristofer Marinus. (1982). *Le Corps Taoiste: Corps Physique, Corps Social* [The Taoist Body: Physical Body, Social Body]. Paris: Fayard.

Scott, W.H. (1984). *Prehispanic Source Material for the Study of Philippine History*. Quezon City, Philippines: New Day.

Scott, John Paul. (1970). Sport and Aggression. In Gerald S. Kenyon (Ed.), *Contemporary Psychology of Sport: Proceedings of the Second International Congress of Sport Psychology* (pp. 11–24). Chicago: Athletic Institute.

Segal, Sandra. (1984, April). Jeet Kune Do: Ten Years Later. *Inside Kung Fu,* pp. 32–37.

Seung, Sahn. (1982). *Only Don't Know.* San Francisco: Four Seasons.

Shaku, Goan. (1907). *Zen to Bushido* [Zen and Bushido]. Tokyo: Koyakan.

Shapiro, Deane H., Jr. (1980). *Meditation: Self-Regulation Strategy and Altered State of Consciousness.* New York: Aldine.

_____. (1982). Overview: Clinical and Physiological Comparison of Meditation with Other Self-Control Strategies. *American Journal of Psychiatry. 139* (3), 267–74.

Shapiro, Deane H., Jr., and Walsh, Roger N. (Eds.). (1984). *Meditation: Classical and Contemporary Perspectives.* New York: Aldine.

Shih, Hu. (1971). *Shen Hui Ho Shang I Chi* [The Works of the Monk Shen-Hui]. Taipei, Taiwan: Hu Shi Chi-Nien-Kuan.

Shim, Sang Kyu. (1974). *Promise and Fulfillment in the Art of Tae Kwon Do.* Detroit: N.P.

_____ (1980). *The Making of a Martial Artist.* Detroit, Michigan: Author.

_____ (1984, May). Meditation in the Martial Arts. *Tae Kwon Do Times,* pp. 30–34.

Silliphant, Stirling. (1970). *The Silent Flute.* N.P.: Pingree-Panpiper Productions.

Sinor, Denis. (1981). The Inner Asian Warriors. *Journal of the American Oriental Society, 101,* 133–44.

Skoss, Meik. (1979a, April). Kuthu Varusai In Penang, Malaysia. *Hoplos,* 1–2.

_____ (1979b, July). Kuthu Varusai In Penang, Malaysia (Part II of II). *Hoplos,* 1–2.

Smith, Bardwell L. (1981). The Pagan Period (1044–1287): A Bibliographic Note. *Contributions to Asian Studies, 16,* 112–30.

Smith, Robert W. (1967). *Pa-Kua: Chinese Boxing for Fitness and Self-Defense.* Tokyo, Japan: Kodansha International.

Smith, Robert W. (1974b). *Hsing-I: Chinese Mind-Body Boxing.* New York: Kodansha International.

Smith, Robert W., and Pittman, Allen. (1990). *Hsing-I: Chinese Internal Boxing.* Tokyo, Japan: Charles E. Tuttle.

Smith, Robert W. (1990). *Pa-Kua: Eight Trigrams Boxing.* Tokyo, Japan: Charles E. Tuttle.

Son, Duk Sung, and Clark, Robert J. (1968). *Korean Karate: The Art of Tae Kwon Do.* Englewood Cliffs, New Jersey: Prentice-Hall.

Sreedharan Nair, Chirakkal T. (1963). *Kalarippayarra.* Cannanore: Cannanore Printing.

Staal, Frits. (1983–84). Indian Concepts of the Body. *Somatics, 4* (3), 31–41.

_____. (no date). *The Martial Arts of India.* Unpublished Book.

Stacton, David. (1958). *Segaki.* New York: Pantheon.

Stange, Paul. (1981). The Sumarah Movement In Javanese Mysticism (Doctoral Dissertation, University of Wisconsin, Madison, Department of History, 1980). *Dissertation Abstracts International, 42,* 334A.

_____. (1984). The Logic of Rasa In Java. *Indonesia, 38,* 113–34.

Staples, Michael P., and Chan, Anthony K. (1976). *Wu Shu of China.* San Francisco, California: Brendan Lai's Supply Company (Distributor).

Stark, Claude Alan. (1974). *God of All: Sri Ramakrishna's Approach to Religious Plurality.* Cape Cod, Massachusetts: Claude Stark.

Stein, R. A. (1971). Illumination Subite ou Saisie Simultanée: Note sur la Terminologie Chinoise et Tibetaine [Sudden Enlightenment or Simultaneous Grasp: Note on Chinese and Tibetan Terminology]. *Revue de l'Histoire des Religions, 179,* 3–30.

Stewart, John. (1980, November). Editorial Perspective. *Black Belt,* p. 6.

Stockmann, Hardy. (1979). *Thai Boxing/Muay Thai: The Art of Siamese Un-Armed Combat.* Bangkok: Editions Duang Kamol.

_____. (1982, September). Krabi Krabong: The Art of Siamese Sword and Stick Fighting. *Lookeast,* pp. 37–40.

Suh, In Hyuk. (1986, April). The Korean Conscience: Impression by Deception. *Inside Kung Fu,* pp. 26, 29.

Suh, In Sun. (1982). *Kuk Sool* (2nd Ed.). Pusan, Korea: Sports Life Company.

Suh, Sung Sool. (no date). *A Brief Introduction to Kuk Sool Won.* Unpublished Manuscript.

Suk, Do-ryun. (1964a). Sun Buddhism in Korea (Pt. 1). *Korea Journal, 4* (1), 34–40.

_____. (1964b). Sun Buddhism in Korea (Pt. 2). *Korea Journal, 4* (3), 41–47.

Sun Tzu. (1963). *The Art of War* (Samuel B. Griffith, Trans.). Oxford: Clarendon Press.

Suzuki, Daisetz Teitaro. (1930). *Studies in the Lankavatara Sutra*. London: George Routledge and Sons.

————. (1932). *The Lankavatara Sutra*. London: George Routledge and Sons.

————. (1959). *Zen and Japanese Culture*. New York: Pantheon Books.

Swearer, Donald K. (1987). Arhat. In Mircea Eliade (Ed.), *The Encyclopedia of Religion* (Vol. 1, pp. 403–5). New York: Macmillan.

Tajima, R. (1959). *Les Deux Grands Mandalas et la Doctrine de l'Esoterism Shingon* [The Two Great Mandalas and the Doctrine of Shingon Esoterism]. Paris: Presses Universitaires De France.

Tambiah, Stanley Jeyaraja. (1984). *The Buddhist Saints of the Forest and the Cult of Amulets*. Cambridge: Cambridge University Press. (Series: Cambridge Studies In Social Anthropology, Vol. 49).

Tamura, Encho. (1974). The Influence of Silla Buddhism on Japan During the Asuka-Hakuho Period. In Chun Shin-Yong (Ed.), *Buddhist Culture in Korea* (pp. 55–79). Seoul, Korea: International Cultural Foundation.

Tamura, Yoshiro. (1987). Tendaishu. In Mircea Eliade (Ed.), *The Encyclopedia of Religion* (Vol. 14, pp. 396–401). New York: Macmillan.

Tang, Zi-Chang (Trans.). (1969). *Principles of Conflict: Recompilation and New English Translation with Annotation on Sun Zi's Art of War*. San Rafael, California: T.C. Press.

Tao-hsüan. (1890). *Hsü Kao Seng Chuan* (10 Vols.) [Biographies of Famous Buddhist Monks]. N.P.: Chiang-Pei Book Printing Store.

Tao Tsang (1, 120 vols.) *[Daoist Canon]*. (1924-1926). Shanghai: Commercial Press.

Tao-yuan. (1935). *Ching Te Ch'uan Têng Lu* (10 Vols.) [Records of the Transmission of the Lamp]. Shanghai: Commercial Press.

Tart, Charles T. (1971). A Psychologist's Experience with Transcendental Meditation. *Journal of Transpersonal Psychology, 3* (2), 135–40.

Tart, Charles T. (1975a). *States of Consciousness*. New York: E. P. Dutton.

————. (Ed.). (1975b). *Transpersonal Psychologies*. New York: Harper and Row.

Taylor, Rodney L. (1983). The Sudden/Gradual Paradigm and Neo-Confucian Mind-Cultivation. *Philosophy East and West, 33* (1), 17–34.

The Martial Concept. (1980, June). *Hoplos,* 3–4.

The Oxford English Dictionary. (1933). Oxford: Clarendon Press.

Thirer, Joel, and Grabiner, Mark D. (1980). Self-Actualization Through Zen and the Martial Arts. *Review of Sport and Leisure,* 5, 79–92.

Thomas, Bruce. (1994). *Bruce Lee: Fighitng Spirit.* Berkeley, California: Frog Ltd.

Toshikaga, Asakura. (1982). The Seventeen Articles of Asakura Toshikaga. In William Scott Wilson (Ed.), *Ideals of the Samurai* (pp. 65–72). Burbank, California: Ohara.

Tucci, Guiseppe. (1923). "Studio Comparativo Fra le Tre Versioni Cinese e il Testo Sanscrito del I e II Capitolo del Lankavatara" [Comparative Study Between Three Chinese Versions and the Sanskrit Text of the First and Second Chapter of the Lankavatara]. Atti Della R. Accademia Nazionale del Lincei (Rome), 5th Series; *Memorie della Classe Discienze Morali, Storiche I Filologiche, Vol. 17,* pp. 169–207.

Ueshiba, Kisshomaru. (1977). *Aikido Kaiso Ueshiba Morihei Den* [Biography of Ueshiba Morihei, Originator of Aikido]. Tokyo, Japan: Kodansha.

Ueshiba, Morihei. (1985a). "Accord with the Totality of the Universe." In Richard Strozzi Heckler (Ed.), *Aikido and the New Warrior* (pp. 23–29). Berkeley, California: North Atlantic Books.

————. (1985b). Excerpts from the Writings and Transcribed Lectures of the Founder, Morihei Ueshiba. In Richard Strozzi Heckler (Ed.), *Aikido and the New Warrior* (pp. 30–33). Berkeley, California: North Atlantic Books.

Ui, Hakuju. (1941). *Zenshushi Kenkyu (Vol. 2)* [Studies in the History of the Zen School]. Tokyo: Iwanami.

Uyehara, Mito. (1988). *Bruce Lee: The Incomparable Fighter.* Santa Clarita, California: Ohara.

Uyeshiba, Kisshomaru. (1974). *Aikido.* Tokyo: Hozansha.

Uyeshiba, Morihei. (1968). *Aikido.* New Jersey: Wehman.

Uzawa, Yoshiyuki. (1990). The Relation of Ethics to Budo and Bushido in Japan. In Minoru Kiyota and Hideaki Kinoshita (Eds.), *Japanese Martial Arts and American Sports: Cross Cultural Perspectives on Means to Personal Growth* (pp. 41–52). Tokyo: Nihon University Press.

Vaughan, Frances. (1983). A Question of Balance: Health and Pathology in New Religious Movements. *Journal of Humanistic Psychology,* 23 (3), 20–41.

Vunak, Paul. (1985, November). The Creation of the Formless Form:

Bruce Lee and the Non-Structure of Jeet Kune Do. *Inside Kung Fu,* pp. 68–73.

Walsh, Roger. (1977). Initial Meditative Experiences: I. *Journal of Transpersonal Psychology, 9,* 151–92.

_____. (1978). Initial Meditative Experiences: II. *Journal of Transpersonal Psychology, 10,* 1–28.

Walsh, Roger, and Shapiro, Deane H. (1983). *Beyond Health and Normality: Explorations of Exceptional Psychological Well-being.* New York: Van Nostrand Reinhold.

Walsh, Roger, and Vaughan, Frances (Eds.). (1980). *Beyond Ego: Transpersonal Dimensions in Psychology.* Los Angeles, California: J. P. Tarcher.

Warner, Gordon, and Draeger, Donn F. (1982). *Japanese Swordsmanship: Technique and Practice.* New York: John Weatherhill.

Watatani, Kiyoshi, and Yamada, Tadachika (Eds.). (1969). *Bugei Ryuha Daijiten* [Comprehensive Dictionary of Classical Martial Arts Traditions] (Rev. Ed.). Tokyo: Shin Jinbutsu Oraisha.

_____. (Eds.). (1978). *Zoho Daikaitei Bugei Ryuha Daijiten* [Enlarged and Greatly Revised Great Encyclopedia of Martial Arts Systems/Traditions]. Tokyo: Tokyo Kopi Shuppambu.

Watson, I. K. (1977). From Karma to Moksha. *Journal of Dharma, 2* (1), 7–21.

Webb, Clement Charles Julian. (1916). *Group Theories of Religion and the Individual.* New York: Macmillan.

Welch, Holmes. (1957). *Taoism: The Parting of the Way.* Boston: Beacon Press.

Welwood, John. (1983). On Spiritual Authority: Genuine and Counterfeit. *Journal of Humanistic Psychology, 23* (3), 42–60.

Wertz, Spencer K. (1977). Zen, Yoga, and Sports: Eastern Philosophy for Western Athletes. *Journal of the Philosophy of Sport, 4,* 68–82.

Wilber, Ken. (1986). The Spectrum of Psychopathology. In Ken Wilber, Jack Engler, and Daniel P. Brown (Eds.), *Transformations of Consciousness: Conventional and Contemplative Perspectives on Development* (pp. 107–26). Boston: New Science Library.

Wilber, Ken, Engler, Jack, and Brown, Daniel P. (1986). *Transformations of Consciousness: Conventional and Contemplative Perspectives on Development.* Boston: New Science Library.

Wile, Douglas. (in press). *Lost T'ai-Chi Classics from the Late Ch'ing Dynasty.* New York: State University of New York Press.

Wiley, Mark V. (1994a). *Filipino Martial Arts: Cabales Serrada Escrima.* Tokyo, Japan: Charles E. Tuttle.

_____. (1994b). Classical Eskrima: The Evolution and Etymology of a Filipino Fencing Form. *Journal of Asian Martial Arts, 3* (2), 72–89.

_____. (1994c). Silat Kebatinan as an Expression of Mysticism and Martial Culture in Southeast Asia. *Journal of Asian Martial Arts, 3* (4), 37–44.

_____. (in press). *Filipino Martial Culture.* Tokyo, Japan: Charles E. Tuttle.

Wiley, Mark V., Maliszewski, Michael, and Purpora, Douglas V. (in press). Talahib-Marga: A Contemporary, Cross-cultural Martial meditative Discipline. *Journal of Asian Martial Arts.*

Wilson, James (1994). Chasing the Magic: Mysticism and the Martial Arts on the Island of Java. *Journal of Asian Martial Arts, 2* (2).

Wong, Douglas. (1976). *The Deceptive Hands of Wing Chun.* Hollywood, California: Unique.

Wong, James I. (Ed.). (1978). *A Source Book in the Chinese Martial Arts: History, Philosophy, Systems and Styles (Vol. 1).* Stockton, California: Koinonia Productions.

_____. (1979a). *A Source Book in the Chinese Martial Arts: Medicine, Meditation, and Military History (Vol. 2).* Stockton, California: Koinonia Productions.

Wong, Shui-hon. (1979). The Cult of Chang San-Feng. *Journal of Oriental Studies, 17* (1 and 2), 10–53.

Yamaguchi, Gogen. (1966). *Karate: Goju-Ryu by the Cat* (Gosei Yamaguchi, Trans.). Tokyo: International Karate-Do Goju-kai.

Yampolsky, Philip B. (Trans.). (1967). *The Platform Sutra of the Sixth Patriarch.* New York: Columbia University Press.

_____. (1971). *The Zen Master Hakuin: Selected Writings.* New York: Columbia University Press.

Yang, Chu-dong. (1957). *Koga Yon'gu* [Research on Ancient Songs]. Seoul: N.P.

Yang, Kep P., and Henderson, Gregory. (1958). An Outline History of Korean Confucianism. Part I: The Early Period and Yi Confucianism. *Journal of Asian Studies, 18* (1), 81–101.

_____. (1959). An Outline History of Korean Confucianism. Part II: The Schools of Yi Confucianism. *Journal of Asian Studies, 18* (1), 81–101.

Yi, Shaowu. (1983, October). Wushu as Seen in Dunhuang Murals. *China Sports*, pp. 24–25.

Young, Robert W. (1993). The History and Development of Tae Kyon. *Journal of Asian Martial Arts, 2* (2), 44–59.

Yu, Yang-shih. (1964–65). Life and Immortality in the Mind of Han China. *Harvard Journal of Asiatic Studies, 25,* 80–122.

Yuasa, Yasuo. (1993). *The Body, Self-Cultivation and Ki-Energy.* Albany, New York: State University of New Yoek Press.

Zalle, Maurice. (1969). Hu Shih and Chinese Philosophy. In K.H. Chen (Ed.), *Chan's Essays.* N.P.: Oriental Society.

Zarrilli, Phillip B. (1978). "Kalarippayatt" and the Performing Artist East and West, Past, Present, Future (Doctoral Dissertation, University of Minnesota). *Dissertation Abstracts International, 39,* 543A.

_____. (1979). Kalarippayatt, Martial Art of Kerala. *The Drama Review, 23* (2), 113–24.

_____. (1984). "Doing the Exercise": The In-Body Transmission of Performance Knowledge in a Traditional Martial Art. *Asian Theatre Journal, 1* (2), 191–206.

_____. (1989 a). Between Text and Embodied Practice: Writing and Reading in a South Indian Martial Tradition. In A. L. Dallapiccola (Ed.), *Shastric Tradition in India* (pp. 415–24). Stuttgart: Franz Steiner Verlag.

_____. (1989b). Three Bodies of Practice in a Traditional South Indian Martial Art. *Social Science and Medicine, 28,* 1289–309.

_____. (Ed.). (in press a). *Martial Arts in Actor Training.* Unpublished Manuscript.

Zarrilli, Phillip B. (1992a). To Heal and/or Harm: The Vital Spots (Marmmam/ Varmam) in Two South Indian Martial Traditions Part I: Focus on Kerala's Kalarippayattu. *Journal of Asian Martial Arts, 1* (1), 36–67.

_____. (1992b). To Heal and/or Harm: The Vital Spots (Marmmam/ Varmam) in Two South Indian Martial Traditions Part II: Focus on the Tamil Art of Varma Ati. *Journal of Asian Martial Arts, 1* (2), 1–15.

_____. (in press b). *When the Body Becomes "All Eyes": Practice, Paradigms and Representations of Power in a South Indian Martial Art.* New Delhi, India: Oxford University Press.

❖ Index ❖

Photo Credits

Michael Maliszewski received his Ph.D. in psychology from the University of Chicago. He has held a number of positions at the University of Chicago and has conducted research and published in a variety of areas ranging from medicine to religious studies. He is currently affiliated with Harvard Medical School. Since 1970, he has studied a variety of different martial arts and became a certified instructor in Kobujutsu, Modified Wing Chun, and Cabales Serrada Escrima. His formal meditation practice has included the study of Theravada Buddhism, Tibetan Vajrayana, Tantric Yoga, and Soto Zen, among other systems. He has also traveled throughout much of Asia to study under and interview masters of martial arts and meditative traditions. Included among his publications in the martial arts are articles that have appeared in the *Journal of Asian Martial Arts* where he also serves as an associate editor.